# Growing Up In Olcott Park

By
Ardys Hawkinson Nelson

**Growing Up in Olcott Park**
Copyright @ 1998 by Ardys Nelson
Published by **Cal Creek Publishing**
Walnut Creek, California
FAX #: 925-933-5216

Cover and Illustration by **Kari Skahill,**
Upland, California

All rights reserved. No part of this publication may be reproduced, stored in a retrieval system or transmitted in any way by any means, electronic, mechanical, photocopy, recording or otherwise, without the prior permission of the publisher, except as provided by USA copyright law.

Printed in the U.S.A.

ISBN 0-9664131-0-5 (pbk.)

# DEDICATION

*In Admiration for and in Memory of*

*Daddy, Mother and Carol, my First Loves*

and

The Dedicated Men who served as Superintendents of Parks and who, with their staffs and the support of the many various Park Commissions and Citizens of Virginia, Minnesota, envisioned, crafted and maintained one of the premier places of fun and beauty in Northern Minnesota, Olcott Park.

<u>Virginia Park Superintendents</u>
J. H. Fleming
Edward Philbrick
Alton F. Thayer
Carl Martin Hawkinson
Walter W. Nelson
George Pepelnjak
Elroy Ornberg
John Bachman

*Olcott Park Welcomes You*

# CONTENTS

PREFACE ................................................................... 7

A BIT OF THE PAST ................................................ 9

MOVING DAY .......................................................... 21

HELP! HELP! ........................................................... 31

THE ROCK GARDEN ............................................. 43

THE VISITORS ........................................................ 55

CREEP ACROSS THE TRESTLE ......................... 65

THE TWINS .............................................................. 71

BUSTER ..................................................................... 77

THE WINTER FROLIC ........................................... 87

CHANGES ................................................................. 101

WHAT'S HAPPENED SINCE? ............................. 115

*Addendum*: Virginia Tourist Camp ................... 121

Olcott Park House Before 1941

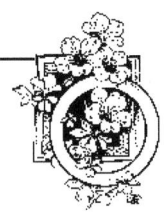

# PREFACE

As a child, I lived in the Olcott Park House in Virginia, Minnesota from 1936 to 1943 when my father, Carl Martin Hawkinson, was Superintendent of Parks. In 1994, the Virginia Area Historical Society and Heritage Museum made the house their home. The Staff and volunteer members of the historical society have gathered numerous photographs and boxes of artifacts collected from citizens, along with much information regarding the Virginia area. All are creatively displayed to invite the visitor to linger and smile. An old log cabin and one of the tourist cabins that stood along Silver Lake have been moved to the museum complex to add authenticity, charm and needed space.

Harry Lamppa, a moving force in the creation and maintenance of the museum, generously opened the house to me on my first return in fifty years. Yes, the rooms were much smaller than I remembered, but they were filled with huge memories of a lovely childhood. The ghosts of sick monkeys, the wonderful park crew, Ida Canossa and her playground activities, and Buster, my horse, drew me back through time and into their playground. And, in my heart I knew that Daddy, Mother and my dear sister Carol were commanding me to write it down.

I did, and now I invite you to smile with me as I tell you about Olcott Park as I remember it was in those years of my childhood. My hope is that you will read my stories to your children and share its bits of history with their grandparents so that they, and you, will visit and be nurtured in a growing appreciation for this magical place of beauty, Olcott Park.

But first, some history.

### MEMORY

My childhood's home I see again,
And sadden with the view;
And still, as memory crowds my brain,
There's pleasure in it, too.

Abraham Lincoln

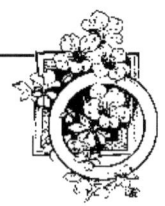

# A BIT OF THE PAST

Olcott Park was named after W. J. Olcott, an officer of the Great Northern Mining Company. The company first leased the 40-acres of land to the City of Virginia in 1905 for one dollar a year, "the city to pay all taxes assessed." In 1910, when my grandfather, Andrew Hawkinson, was mayor, a 10-year lease was drawn and Olcott Park had its official opening on May 11, 1911. In 1920 and 1930, the city re-negotiated a ten-year lease at $10.00 per year, and on June 15, 1939, when my father was Park Superintendent, it purchased Olcott Park from the Oliver Mining Company for $9,015. My roots go deep.

Virginia, whose history is written in the story of lumbering and mining, was named in honor of Alfred E. Humphrey whose home was in the State of Virginia, and who was president of the Virginia Improvement Company who platted the town site in 1892. The Arrowhead Country had belonged to the Colony of Virginia until 1784, although the Indians were in possession by title. The stands of virgin pine, once the home of Ojibway Indians, whom the early trappers interpreted as Chippewa, gave the name added significance.

In the early part of the century, The Virginia and Rainy Lake Lumber Company boasted the largest white pine mill in the world, turning out 225,000,000 feet during its peak year. At the time of my story, W.T.Bailey Lumber Comany, whose first sawmill was built in 1895, still produced 35,000 feet of pine lumber daily.

The city is located in Northeastern Minnesota on the Mesabi Range, a 100-mile long and 1-1/2 to 3-mile wide iron formation dotted with open and underground mines, some extending a half-mile deep. In 1941, the open-pit Missabe Mountain Mine at the east end of Chestnut Street was the largest, single, iron-ore producing mine in the world, shipping 7,000 tons of high grade ore per day.

Almost two thousand years ago the Mound-builders passed this way and remained awhile. In the seventeenth century, French trappers, missionaries and explorers, Radisson and Du Lhut among them, found Sioux in the Arrowhead Country. The Chippewa, coming from the east along the shores of Lake Superior, gradually drove the Sioux to the west and south and probably lived along the shores of Silver Lake. Then, two industries, lumber and mining, attracted thirty-nine different nationality groups to the area.

Lumbermen surged in when the Minnesota legislature chartered a State Road to be built in the Arrowhead Country in 1866. A railroad reached Duluth in 1870, and a year later, the Duluth Ship Canal opened. Lumbering first attracted New Yorkers and New Englanders; then, French and Scots from eastern Canada. Later, Irish, Germans, Scandinavians, Finns, Slavs, Italians, Poles, Greeks, Montenegrans and other Europeans arrived to look for work in the forests, mills and ore mines. Virginia was settled in rich cultural diversity.

# A Bit Of The Past

In Virginia's Finntown, many households lit up the basement sauna for the weekly bath in 1936. On the Northside, Italians bottled heavy 'dago red', Robert Mondavi among them. Lutefisk suppers and pancake breakfasts were enjoyed in Lutheran church basements. Slavanian potica, full of walnuts and brown sugar, was relished by all at Christmastime. Canelakes, the Greeks, made mouth-watering seafoam candy in their candy kitchen on Main Street. Welsh pasties were baked and sold from several kitchens around town and eaten in the mines at lunch time.

Before 1939, when the Weber Carley Bill was passed, local taxation on the Mesabi required the prosperous mining companies to pay more than 95% of all taxes levied. Rich city coffers generously provided services for their populations, and area schools were the most elaborate in the country. As recipients of this favorable tax structure, the six public elementary schools, the junior high school and Roosevelt High School employed educationally well-qualified teachers whose salaries were at the top of the pay scale in Minnesota; $1200 a year. Women teachers were paid less than their male counterparts and were required to remain single.

The tree-lined, grassy boulevards, eighteen-hole golf course, public building lawns, Southside Park and Olcott Park were maintained and developed under the supervision of a Park Superintendent and a governing Park Commission. The parks and broad boulevards throughout the city were initially developed in 1910, and, in the Spring of 1916, the four-bedroom Olcott Park home was moved from a near-by location to its present 40-acre site.

During the years of my father's superintendency, an electric fountain, with landscaped stonework and adjoining three-acre rock garden, was built in Olcott Park. Sprays of water still surge thirty feet into the air and are highlighted in many colors as they change form, reminding some of dancing fireworks. Then, as now, chrysanthemum and begonia shows drew tourists and people from the area to the greenhouse. The smaller Southside Park and Olcott Park bragged Victorian bandstands, where, on Sunday evenings in summer, the City Band gave concerts, alternating between the north and south sides of town. The musicians were each paid five dollars per night.

In 1936, Olcott Park had large, grassy pens for elk, moose, llama, buffalo, white-tail deer and mountain goats. Small animals native to the area, brown and black bear, and monkeys had similarly comfortable accommodations. The city recreation department supervised and provided daily summer game and craft actvities for children in the park's well-equipped playground.

My father was instrumental in the planting of a stand of blue spruce on the west side of Silver Lake in 1941. Plans to develop a Silver Lake Park there were tabled because of the advent of World War II. The park department created a winter "Iron Bowl" sports area in Sliver Pit, one of the non-producing iron ore pits north of town. Near it, about two miles north of Virginia, is the Great Laurentian Divide, the only place in the United States where you can spill a pail of water and part of it will reach Hudson Bay, part the Gulf of St. Lawrence, and part the Gulf of Mexico.

In 1936 the country was recovering from the Great Depression. Franklin Roosevelt was President, and 80,000,000 radio-minded Americans tuned in for his weekly fireside chats regarding the New Deal and his "Rendezvous With Destiny." Margaret Mitchell's *Gone With the Wind* won the Pulitzer Prize. Japan nibbled at China's sovereignty, and King Edward VIII abdicated the English throne for the love of a divorced American, Wallis Simpson.

Adolph Hitler was remilitarizing the Rhineland, giving the world its first inkling of his intentions. Civilians throughout Spain,

# A Bit Of The Past

Loyalists and Rebels, took up arms against each other, and the ugly three-year civil war began. Shirley Temple was an adorable, dimpled child of Hollywood. Bronco Nagurski, a son of Northeastern Minnesota, was the feared All-American tackle and fullback for the Chicago Bears.

It was another time—a safe time in which to grow up in small-town, mid-western America. The city jail hosted a drunk or two on weekends; it also welcomed visitors who couldn't find a room for the night. Mothers, and the Grandmothers who lived with them, canned tomatoes and peaches, using a separate canning stove located in the basement next to the wringer washing machine. Most homes were heated by steam sent through a network of pipes from its municipal source, the Virginia Water and Light Building.

Father was usually the only breadwinner. If a businessman, on days when he didn't go to Rotary or Kiawanis, he ate lunch at home or at Henle's Cafeteria, and walked to work— or took the Lambert Motor Coach's nickel-a-ride city bus that toured the city on the hour. The miners and mill workers carried lunch pails and waited for the noon whistle to wail, reminding them it was lunchtime. It was not necessary to lock your doors; it was also impolite. The community looked after each other's kids. Incomes were similar, and none of us thought we were poor.

Persons, a popular Main Street grocery store, was one of several that delivered groceries ordered by party-line telephones. Noone had heard the words *juvenile delinquency*, and when "Cully" Person scolded me for sampling a Bing cherry in his limited produce department where only seasonal fruits and vegetables were sold, it was the last time in my life I ever thought of stealing anything. When winter came, the rumor was that dogs lifted their legs onto the barrels containing huge slabs of frozen cod that stood outside the store in the freezing temperature. Scandinavians called the fish lutefisk and vied for the windward side of the table when eating the smelly, slippery stuff.

Postcards cost a penny; three cents to mail a letter, but to whom did you write? Practically everyone you knew lived in town.

Movies were popular. Every Saturday in winter, almost every kid in town helped pack one of the three movie theaters to cheer for the men in the white hats. Television had not yet been introduced, but, in addition to two, full-length, black and white movies, Movietone News, and a cartoon or two, the matinee at the Granada Theater featured Hopalong Cassidy and Wild Bill Hickock in weekly serials. Flash Gordon brought us a prophetic look at our future. A kid's admission was ten cents. Popcorn or a candy bar took a whole nickel.

District and Regional basketball tournaments held in the Memorial Building near City Hall stirred the population to frenzy in March. At other times, the "Rec" arena was used for tap and figure skating lessons, hockey games, and curling matches, where sweeping a large, round stone up and down the ice kept the players warm. Friday night "Kit Kat Dances" provided live music of this Big Band Era for dancing high schoolers. Girl Scouts met in their room-with-kitchen on the top floor of the City Hall; Boy Scout troops gathered in basements of their sponsoring churches.

Children played kick-the-can in the streets at night and knew where every crab apple tree in the neighborhood was located—and when they were ripe for raiding. In summer, flags were waved at the annual Fourth of July Parade on Main Street and the Fireworks Show on Silver Lake.

And almost everyone who hadn't already taken up residence for the summer at the family cabin on a nearby lake picnicked in the shaded greenness of Olcott Park, where my story begins.

## MY MOTHER'S PRAYER

As I wandered round the homestead,
Many a dear, familiar spot
Brought within my recollection
Scenes I'd seemingly forgot.

Though the house was held by strangers,
All remained the same within,
Just as when a child I rambled
Up and down and out and in.

T.C. O'Kane

# A PEEK INTO HISTORY

### City Resolution #20, dated April 19, 1910. Vol. 7

"A 10-year lease dated April 1, 1910 for such purposes only, viz: to improve, maintain and use the (above) for a public park and recreation ground.

"Pay all taxes and assessments, general and special. It is agreed that there would be no professional baseball games, or baseball game or athletic contest to which an admission fee is charged.

"No fences built to exclude public (where admission is charged) but fences can be built along boundary lines.

"Never be used for sale, barter or disposal of intoxicating liquors, no structure building booth or tent may be placed for sale of same.

"Surface only—party of 1st part, retains right to iron ore and all other ore, minerals and fossils underneath.

"6 month notice for termination of leasee.

"Signed by Pentecost Mitchel, Vice President, Great Northern Mining Company."

### Letter from Special Auditor, W.M.T. Townes, to Park Commission:

"Recommended to purchase property (Olcott Park) under privately arranged terms, or under condemnation proceedings."

" —*estimated population within 30 years will be 25,000 to 30,000.*"

"*It is easy to see that when the operation of the present owner of this property shall have been closed permanently in this municipality that this City will either lose Olcott Park or else be forced to purchase it at its then high value.*"

### Duluth and St. Louis County — Their Story and People Vol..11. PG. 599 —American Historical Society
1921

"*The City owns 55 acres of park property, in Olcott and Southside Parks, among the finest in the state, records the Minneapolis Daily News. It's Park Board maintains more than 35 miles of boulevards and has planted more than 10,000 trees. Olcott Park is known as one of the playspots of the range. Its zoo is a feature that draws visitors from all sections. It contains elk, deer, grizzly bear, timber wolfs* (sic) *and coyotes; foxes; waterfowl, cavies, and everything to make a complete zoo. All the parks are equipped with playground apparatus, while a wading pool for the children is a feature at Olcott Park. Olcott Park was leased from the Great Northern Mining Company in 1910, for ten years, one of the conditions of lease being that the land was 'to be used strictly for park purposes,' and that no exhibitions for compensation were to be permitted.*"

## Superintendents' Reports to Park Commission

*1925*
*"Monkey House built at east end of park. Four wolf pups purchased at $6.00 each."*

*1928*
*"Greenhouse addition — labor and material, $2,581.49."*
*"Sold elk and deer hides — $722.31."*

*December, 1936*
*"Begonia Display—1100 Tuberous Rooted Begonias Chrysanthemum—4th Annual display in November."*
*"All clergymen were furnished with transportation and responded by announcing the show at their Sunday services. 3,000 people atended."*

*March, 1939*
*"By resolutions adopted by the Virginia Park Commission at its meeting held on July 29, 1938, it was decided to accept the offer of the Oliver Iron Mining Company to sell the City of Virginia 30.05 acres of Olcott Park for $9,015—$4515 payable at once and the balance on delivery of deed on or before August 1, 1939."*
*"Entered into a lease covering 5.28 acres lying immediately south of the premises to be conveyed. (Retained by Oliver Iron Mining Company for right -of-way to the Sauntry Mine)."*

*The Virginia and Rainy Lake Company; once the world's largest white pine mill, closed in 1929.*

*Technical High School Building in 1928*

*Iron Ore Freighter, 1940's*

# MOVING DAY

"I'm probably the luckiest kid in the whole world," I thought. "I'm gonna' live in Olcott Park. I won't have any neighbor kids to play with, but I'll have monkeys, and bear, and deer to feed. Carol and I can play with all those kids who visit the park with their moms and dads. And every day I'll ride the long, curvy slide with the big bump in it." I was so excited. My insides tingled with joy as I raced up the stairs, two at a time.

The breeze that gentled the empty house on the east side of Olcott Park was unusually hot that sticky August day in 1936 and chased us as we ran to choose our bedrooms on the second floor of the big, four-bedroom house. My father had been recently appointed Superintendent of Parks, and the city-owned park house was now our new home.

"I'm the oldest so I get to pick first," I declared, as I pushed my little sister Carol aside and claimed the bedroom that overlooked the greenhouse. I was seven and much older, by seventeen months.

Carol hitched the strap of her blue striped sunsuit and pulled herself up on the window sill of the smaller room across the hall. She looked out the window and smiled. "I want this one, anyway."

From her window, she could see the playground and its "Merry-Whirl," and the Roman fountain with the funny little cherubs blowing water out of their shells.

Two additional bedrooms at the end of the upstairs hall were larger and faced the forty-acre park grounds to the west. The white, hexagon-tiled bathroom at the head of the stairs, with its cold, clawfooted bathtub, was the only other room on the second floor.

Mahogany sleigh beds were soon set up in our rooms. Mother threw in a pile of linens and said, "Here are your sheets, girls. Help each other make your beds so you'll have a place for your dolls when they come."

Probably thinking this task would keep our energetic enthusiasm in check for awhile, she hurried downstairs to direct the movers who were trying to get the baby grand piano into the house. The rounded stone pillars on either side of the entrance steps did not make that an easy job, but the men soon struggled it into the enclosed front porch of the house. With its legs off, the beautiful instrument sat on its side.

Carol and I left our unmade beds and sat watching on the stairs above the scene as the men carried the piano carefully through the front door. After much sweaty maneuvering, they finally placed the piano against the stairway wall of the living room, legs intact..

An overstuffed, dark brown velour davenport was placed against the wall to face the fireplace whose mantle was wide enough to fill with family pictures. I knew the pictures of Grandpa and Grandma Hawkinson would soon be placed there. Grandpa, looking distinguished with his thick, grey hair, bushy eyebrows and long moustache, emigrated in 1880 from Ystad, Sweden and had been mayor of Virginia. Grandma, who emigrated from Trondheim, Norway in 1883, had a huge mole on the left side of her nose. Mother had jokingly told us if we lied we would grow a mole like that, too.

Carol and I wondered what Grandma had lied about to have such a big one.

Grandpa used to have the only hardware store in Virginia. When the town burned down in 1900, the family home and hardware store, with all their contents, were destroyed. Grandpa got a loan and was back in business in a few days. Most of the glass in the re-built city of Virginia was purchased at his new hardware store. When he died in 1926, the entire city closed down for the afternoon so people could attend his funeral.

"Did you get your beds made, girls?" Mother called, spotting us peeking through the rails of the staircase. I mumbled a guilty 'yes' while picking at a hole in my sock.

Probably remembering Grandma's mole, Carol got up to return to her bedroom. I grabbed her ankle and said, "Oh look, Carol. Here comes the radio."

The console RCA Victor radio, with its familiar logo of Nipper barking into a large speaker, was placed against the wall next to the fireplace. It's hinged top protected the Victrola phonograph inside. "Maybe, if we hurry and finish making our beds, we can listen to Little Orphan Annie. I hope Punjab found Daddy Warbucks."

I felt a little uneasy about the previous fib on the stairway and was curious to look in the mirror to see if there was a mole on my face. We ran back to our rooms to tug and pull and try to smooth our beds. No mole was apparent.

"Who gets the dolls?" questioned one of the men who was helping with the move. A large carton was deposited in my room, and I dumped its contents onto the floor. Two Shirley Temple dolls, two large baby dolls and two small Effanbee dolls, with smiles on their faces to match Carol's and mine were placed against the pillows on our high, three-quarter sleigh beds. Books and games were divided, and my attempt to stack some of them into a bookcase resulted in checkers scattering themselves to every corner of my room.

"Uff da," I cried, using the Norwegian lament I heard Mother proclaim in similar situations. "Come here, Carol. Help me with these checkers."

Sitting on the floor of her room putting shoes on her Effanbee, Carol ignored me. I soon had the checkers returned to their box. Chests of drawers holding our clothes arrived and school dresses, coats and snowsuits were hung in the small closets. A picture of a little girl in a satin, smocked dress watching a bluebird in a tree was sent to Carol's room. I held my favorite of a little boy sitting under a treee wishing he were a little rock. Not me. Today I was glad I was me!

We knelt on the radiator cover under the window of my room and looked at the activity below. The greenhouse was filled with lush palms, ferns, cactii and flowers. Park Department trucks were parked on the cinder utility road that ran behind the house and greenhouse.

A chain-link fence extended in an irregular line along the road at the back of the house, from the entrance gate on Ninth Street to the south corner of the park. In the distance, we saw Silver Lake with its swimming beach and tourist cabins and the Duluth, Winnipeg and Pacific railway station at the west end of Main Street.

A curving trestle, spanning one corner of the lake and used by the DW&P Railroad for its "ten ten" evening train between Duluth and Winnipeg, swung toward us . A grassy field stretched from the park east a quarter of a mile to Sixth Avenue, its only occupant a building supply company.

Next to the park, and out of sight from my window, a large, dark brown, vine-covered Oliver Mining Company house faced

# Moving Day

Ninth Street and the Washington Elementary School. The Pellenzes, the mining superintendent and his wife who lived there, were our closest neighbors.

Having forgotten Little Orphan Annie, we looked out from our site on the small hill above the Northeastern Minnesota city of 12,000 people. Off in the distance at the east end of Main Street, we could see Missabe Mountain, the dark red, open ore pit, which was our city's life blood.

We listened to monkeys chattering to each other and the occasional yawn of black bear in their den at the other end of the park. The breeze through the open window smelled of freshly cut grass. We heard the hum of a mobilized lawn mower. A robin hopped and listened for worms. A trellis, covered with clematis vine, stretched to my window.

I put my arm around my little sister, whom I lovingly nicknamed when she was born, and said, "We're really lucky, Coo. I think we're going to like it here. Let's go see the monkeys."

### MOVING

I like to move. There's such a feeling
Of hurrying
and scurrying,
And such a feeling
Of men with trucks and packing cases,
Of kitchen clocks and mother's laces,
Dusters, dishes, books and vases,
Toys and pans and candles.

Eunice Tietjens

# A PEEK INTO HISTORY

### An Epoch of Progress: Illustrated supplement to "The Daily Virginian," 1915.

*"Among the company's donations to the city of Virginia should be noted the ground occupied by Olcott Park, a tract of 40 acres or more which is located in a section of the city readily reached by all its inhabitants." (Great Northern Mining Company)*

### Superintendents' Reports to Park Commission

*March, 1915*
*"Park Gardens used to raise vegetables for animals:*
*235 bushels potatoes      55 bushels mangals*
*50 bushels bagas           5 bushels turnips*
*130 bushels carrots        4 ton cabbage*
*55 bushels potatoes distributed to needy poor through Association Charities and Salvation Army.*

<u>Animals in Zoo</u>
*2 red-faced apes           12 cavies*
*7 rhesus monkeys           1 male coyote*
*25 mixed guinea pigs       2 black bear*
*ringtail monkeys           1 grizzly bear*
*2 foxes*

*March, 1916*
"*In the Spring, the residence was moved. Large living room made out of two small rooms, with stairway leading to a second story. Fireplace built. Old residence walls and basement were used as nucleus for a fountain and pool.*"

"*Stone entrances for Olcott Park constructed at cost of $1995.00.*"

*March, 1917*
"*Improvement and repairs made to residence—including plumbing, heating, sewers, extending bath, basement floor, chimney & fireplace—cost $667.88.*"

*April 2, 1917*
"*In no one year has so much real construction work been accomplished, as has taken place during the year ending March 31.*
"*The re-arrangement of Olcott Park in conformity with the design of the Landscape Architect was perhaps the most notable feature.*"

*March, 1929*
"*A memorial fountain was placed in the park by Mrs. Katherine Roman in memory of her husband Joseph.*"

*March, 1930*
"*Olcott Park leased by Great Northen Mining Company to Virginia for park purposes for 10 years from 4/1/30, the city to pay all taxes assessed.*"

*March, 1934*
*"The main object was the giving of relief, whereby those so employed would be considered gainfully employed." (C.W.A. Federal Grant: $46,773.00).*

*March, 1936*
*"The big attraction is spelled MONKEY, and these animals on their newly constructed ISLAND are the happiest and livliest bunch of animals anywhere. Their antics are witnessed by thousands of visitors—and their antics the past year caused many a good laugh by the older folks, as well as the young. The number of visitors to this particular part of the park played havoc with our roads, and will necessitate considerable repairs this coming year."*

## Virginia Daily Enterprise

*June, 1936*
*"Hawkinson tells Rotary Club of Park's history—The city's first park was started in 1905—cost of operations in 1907 was $1,019 while the current year's budget is approximately $40,000. All park areas are leased properties. Use of the parks has steadily increased with the passing of each year. The trend towards the out-of-doors is natural in man, the speaker asserted. This has been appreciated in the planning of American cities, and especially during the past half-century have parks received more and more attention in the cities."*

*Moving Day*

"*Mr. Hawkinson declared that the animals at Olcott Park prove a source of pleasure to most of the visitors, monkey island in particular receiving great attention. At the present time, Olcott Park has elk, native deer, black deer, white deer, buffalo, mountain sheep, beaver, black and brown bear, black squirrels and monkeys.*"

*March 31, 1940*
"*Final payment on Olcott Park Purchase was made on June 16, 1939.*"

*Monkey Island was a favorite place*

# HELP! HELP!

Carol and I explored every inch and cranny of the 40-acre park that summer and fall. Each day was an adventure. After eating our dishes of oatmeal in the morning that Daddy made for us, we tagged along after Frank Persons, the animal caretaker, or joined other children on the playground.

The Mesabi Iron Range was basically populated by hard-working, first and second generation people who came to this rugged country as lumbermen and miners. Children of many nationality backgrounds blended and enjoyed each others' rich, cultural heritages. Someone later said the only discrimination in Virginia was whether you lived on the Northside or the Southside of town. Many children came into the public kindergartens speaking no English, but all learned before they left. They joyfully shared a common language in Olcott Park.

Carol and I played with the children who visited the playground where we made sand castles in the large sandboxes and pushed each other on the high swings. Sometimes, we took our dolls or paper dolls to the lawn between the house and the greenhouse or watched Charlie West plant and weed flower beds. Croquet was a favorite game, and we spent hours hitting the wooden balls with their different colored stripes through the wickets. We visited Monkey Island every day during the summer. When September's cooler days arrived, the monkeys were shipped back to the supplier.

Winter was a quiet time for all residents of the park. The monkeys went south, the bear hibernated, and the gardens were covered with snow. Sundown arrived in the late afternoon and urged us inside toward the fireplace.

The snowfall of 1936 was heavy. Pine trees stretched toward the sun, begging to be warmed a bit. Snow covered their spreading branches and, when warmed, slid to the ground with a swish, or sprayed each spurt of breeze with fine, white flecks of coldness.

One blizzardy morning, the local radio station broadcast that the Virginia schools would be closed for a snow holiday. The temperature and driving conditions made it too hazardous for the buses to pick up the children who lived in the locations and on the farms, and the local children who walked to school could not safely navigate the snowdrifts and frigid conditions. Snow holidays, which usually occured at least once a year, were good news for the kids. We all listened attentively to the radio on especially blustery school mornings, hoping that a snow holiday would be delclared by our school superintendent. When we heard the announcement, Carol and I were ecstatic.

Mother, who was not as happy about the news, said, "When you have cleaned up the mess in your bedrooms, the rest of the day is yours to do what you want." She went back to the sink to wash and wipe the dirty breakfast dishes.

It was no easy task, but when we had done a passable job on our bedrooms, Carol and I decided to roller skate in the L-shaped basement where we skated around the posts and under the clotheslines without knocking jars of canned tomatoes, green beans and peaches off their shelves.

Sonja Henie, the Olympic ice-skating champion, was a new movie star. We unsuccessfully tried to copy her gracefulness on the metal roller skates, which we strapped to our shoes and tightened with large keys. After awhile, we got bored and took our bruised knees upstairs.

Listening to us fight over what radio programs to listen to, what paper dolls to play with, and whose turn it was in jacks, Mother looked at the large thermometer outside the small window of the kitchen and said, "It looks like it's warmed up a bit. I can't stand listening to you two fight any longer. Why don't you put on your snowsuits and go outside and play until dinner?"

Bundled up in our snowsuits and boots, we got our sled from the garage and pulled it down the road to a high, well-packed snowbank near Monkey Island. About the only traffic there in winter was Frank Person's black pickup that he used when he fed the animals. Our snow boots crunched stairs into the side of the bank, and we pulled the sled to the top. From there, we slid down and across the road to the opposite side. Sliding on the high snowbank was fun and occupied us for a long time.

After awhile, Carol said, "I know what we can do. Let's make snow fairies." The fresh, powdery snow was ideal for snow fairies. We didn't call them angels like some kids did because angels are warm. The bright, newly-fallen snow was ideal for our icy, snow fairies.

We left the sled by the snowbank and struggled through the deep snow to a flat area where the surface lay smooth and untouched. Standing a few feet apart from each other, we fell straight back into the soft snow. Lying there, we pushed our arms from our sides to our heads and down again to make wings in the the snow. Our spreading legs made long dresses for our fairies. Resting in the cold and peaceful softness, we listened. Everything was still, except the wind that blew swirls of snow before it as it hustled through the park.

"I could fall asleep here," said Carol, looking up at the pale blue, and now cloudless, sky. "It's so comfortable."

Knowing the danger of falling asleep in the snow I said, "Come on, get up. We've got room to make a million fairies here."

I stretched to a space next to my first fairy and, falling backward, made another one. Carol joined me, and soon we had the clearing between the garage and Monkey Island filled with snow fairies.

Lying on my back in the snow, I could see the tall castle on Monkey Island. The monkeys had been sent south for the winter and the castle invited exploration. Inspired, but not wanting to mess up my latest fairy's skirts, I carefully got up and said, "Coo, I've got a really great idea. Let's explore the castle on Monkey Island and find out what it's like inside. The snow is almost to the top of the moat. Come on."

We had recently spent a dime of our allowances to see Freddie Barholomew in *Little Lord Fauntelroy* at the Garrick Theater. The little lord lived in a real English castle so it wasn't hard to persuade Carol, who was as curious as I. The moat surrounding the castle on the island was piled deep with snow, and we were both eager to begin the exploration. The three-foot fence around the outer wall of the island was, in some places, covered with drifts. We struggled over it on our stomachs and lay looking into the moat.

"Looks easy to me," Carol said. "You go first."

I stood on the ledge of the wall and jumped into the soft snow. "Come on, Coo. It's fun." She followed me in, and we scrambled up the sides of the castle.

We explored and climbed around the stone castle's slippery, sloping sides. We peered into the small openings to the small room inside where, in summer, the monkeys sat watching their visitors. We were princesses; this was our castle. We make-believed in Fauntelroy's world until the shadows of the pine trees lay very long on the snow.

"Mother said she was going to make chop suey for dinner, Ardys. Let's go home. It's getting dark, and I'm getting hungry." Carol didn't like chop suey but the accompanying rice was one of her favorite foods. She trudged through the deep snow that filled the moat and reached for the edge of the wall.

Getting in had been easy. Getting out wasn't. There was no way we could reach the top of the wall surrounding the moat and pull ourselves up. The snow, piled so high, was deceivingly soft, and we sunk into it up to our waists. Moving around the snow-filled moat, we tried to stand on the highest drifts, which showed some possibility of escape. There's got to be a way to get out of here, I thought to myself as I looked around the island, but I could spot nothing that we could use to help us get out.

"Here, Coo. Get on my shoulders and pull yourself up," I said, hopefully. But, when she got on my shoulders, I couldn't get through the heavy snow without sinking in and falling. She couldn't reach the top edge of the wall.

I knelt down and said, "Here, I'll make a place in my hands for your foot. I'll lift you up, and you can go for help." That didn't work, either. Carol just wasn't tall enough to reach the top of the wall. She held her hands for me to use as a step, but we both fell back into the snow.

"You have dumb ideas, Ardys. I don't know why I ever jumped in here, anyway. How are we going to get out, Smarty Ardy?" Carol complained.

The shadows lay black on the white, white snow and stretched even longer than before. There were no knights in shining armor to rescue us from our snowy castle. I was worried. We climbed up the side of the castle to look again for boxes or something on which to stand. It was empty, except for a small piece of frozen banana peel.

"Yell, that's what we'll do. We'll yell, and someone will hear us," returned Smarty Ardy. Defiantly. No one was going to call my ideas dumb.

"Fat chance anyone's gonna' hear us," Carol countered. "Everyone has gone home by now. You and your dumb ideas." It was after four-thirty, and the park employees' work day had ended. Absolutely no one was around to see or hear us. Apparently, Freddie Bartholomew had had no problems with snow. His moat had been filled with water.

"Help! Help! We're in the Monkey Island. Help! Help!" we yelled. The white mountain sheep, standing on top of their rocky hill next to us, watched with detached interest.

The sun completed its journey across the darkening sky. It was cold and very quiet. We were scared. Who would ever think to look for us in the deserted Monkey Island? The snow fairies lay next to our prison, like an army of useless soldiers.

In the house, Mother was chopping celery for chop suey. She noticed it was dark, but reasoned we were probably with Daddy, or in the greenhouse where we often played steal-the-pack with Mr. Niemi. John Niemi was the night watchman who had worked in the park for years. We pestered him mercilessly, but shared a mutual affection.

When Daddy came home without us and heard we weren't home, he said he would go down the road to the greenhouse and bring us back for dinner.

Mr. Niemi was in the greenhouse. Alone. With the sun having set, it was getting very cold outside. Daddy was concerned and

*Help! Help!*

explained the situation to Mr. Niemi. They decided to drive in different directions to look for us. By now, two of the main roads in the park had been plowed.

We heard their horns honking and continued to yell as we sat perched on a ledge of the castle in Monkey Island. "Help! Here we are. We're in Monkey Island. Help! Help!" There was no moon; it was very dark. Our feet and hands were freezing. "Help Help!"

Mr. Niemi found us a short time later. Driving slowly and using his truck's night watchman's search lights, he spotted our abandoned sled and the bivouacking army of fairies.

He stopped his truck and heard us yell, "Help! Help! We're in the Monkey Island. Help! Help!"

Soon, he was reaching over the wall to pull two frightened, embarrassed and very cold little girls up and out of the snowy moat. We hugged him and climbed into his truck. For once, we weren't jabbering. He brought us home, shivering, to our worried mother.

After we had been properly scolded, we were sent upstairs to take hot baths before dinner. Even hungrier now, Coo ate a bowlful of rice with cinnamon and sugar, and even tried the chop suey, which I loved. Although we were sent to bed to think about what we had done and how dangerous it was, my thoughts were magically filled with fairy princesses and gallant knights who lived in stone castles surrounded by water-filled moats. Just like Freddie Bartholomew.

Everyone else seemed to get a good laugh from our misadventure, but Carol and I didn't laugh. We remembered the cold and the feelings of helplessness we felt that evening in our frigid castle. When the park crews saw us, they teased and asked us what it was like living on Monkey Island. Already a friend, Mr. Niemi was now our hero, our gallant knight.

For at least a year after that, whenever we had a sister fight, our exasperated Mother would say, "Stop that or I'll send you both back to Monkey Island and tell Mr. Niemi to leave you there."

No way. Coo was right. Jumping into a snow-filled Monkey Island was one of Smarty Ardy's dumber ideas.

### THE FIRST SNOWFALL

The snow had begun in the gloaming,
And busily all the night
Had been heaping field and highway
With a silence deep and white.

Every pine and fir and hemlock
Wore ermine too dear for an earl,
And the poorest twig on the elm tree
Was ridged inch deep with pearl.

J. H. Fleming,
First Park Superintendent

*Carol and Ardys
in front of Olcott Park House,
1938*

# A PEEK INTO HISTORY

### Superintendents' Reports to Park Commission

*March, 1934*
"Regarding rock enclosure for housing of Mountain Sheep: Stone Masons putting our native rock into a fairly large size rock house, built upon a knoll just east of animal enclosures."
"Mountain Sheep ordered from Banff National Park in Canada."

*March, 1935*
"Monkey Island was constructed with CWA labor and ERA assistance. It is oval shaped, 310 feet in circumference. Around outer edge is a heavy wall of solid masonary, and in the bottom a floor of a very good mixture of concrete, with necessary plumbing for fresh water and outlets to drain and keep it in sanitary condition. There is a room inside of Castle, with doors and window outlets. Between castle and wall is a lake of water which the monkeys cannot escape to get off the island. Rope ladders, trees, boats, rafts and other contrivances are at their disposal."
"A cement walk 310 feet long and 6 feet wide, circles the bowl-shaped enclosure. Steel picket fence—3" high—safeguards the spectators from being pushed into the artificial lake."
"Rock enclosure for housing Mountain Sheep being built. Stone Masons putting our native rock into a fairly large size rock house, built upon a knoll just east of animal enclosures."

*January, 1941*
"The only Mountain Sheep we had left died during the month. The symptoms were the same as in previous deaths. A severe diarrhea was noted in all cases. The cause can be attributed to the necessity of keeping these animals in too close quarters and inbreeding. In their natural habitat, lichens and scant evergreen plants form a large part of their diet. These are not available in the food supply we must use and accounts for the lowered resistance of the Mountain Sheep. The older pair lived their natural life span, for sheep in captivity. The sheep born in the park lacked the ruggedness of the older pair that were imported from the Canadian Rockies."

*September, 1942*
"The sheep enclosure was converted into a rabbit pen."

*April, 1943*
"We have had considerable trouble with the rabbits in the Monkey Island. Dogs, cats and kids took quite a toll of the young. This has become quite serious since meat has been rationed."

## **Virginia Daily Enterprise**

"Total Snowfall, October to February:
1934-35—57 ft. 50 in.
1935-36—43 ft. 20 in.
1936-37—97 ft. 10 in.
1937-38—52 ft. 70 in.
1938-39—68 ft. 40 in.

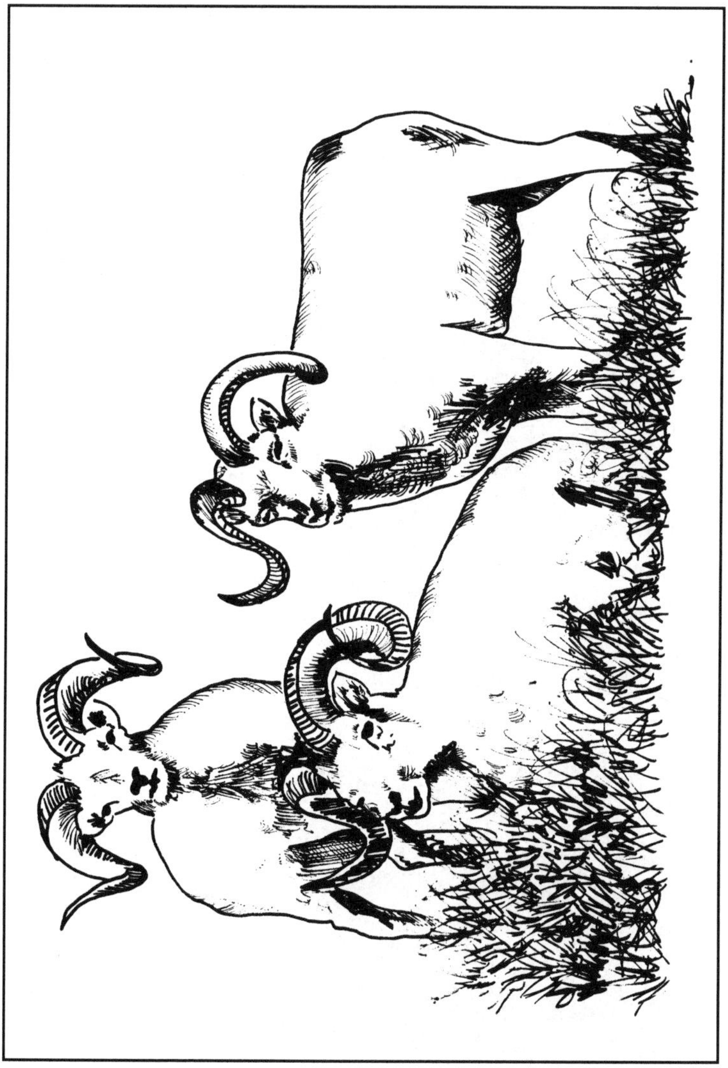

Olcott Park Bandstand

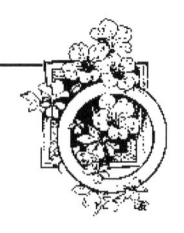

# THE ROCK GARDEN

Virginia hummed with excitement. The Minnesota American Legion Convention convened this week in the city. Gunnar Peterson, Olcott Park's long-time, respected florist, had designed and planted a special Legion floral display next to the center road in Olcott Park. All of the boulevards and both parks were trimmed and planted in preparation for the crowds expected to visit the city.

The annual Begonia Show in the Olcott greenhouse was extended for the convention and throngs of people from all over the Range came to see the hundreds of waxy blooms of many varied colors and shapes. A gala parade was planned for Saturday, with high school bands coming from all over Minnesota. Main Street merchants had decorated their storefronts with flags and bunting in red, white and blue.

Daddy was very busy all week directing the completion of the three-acre rock garden in the center of Olcott Park, which included an electric fountain and decorative plantings. The garden had been started two years before, and the whole town was anticipating tomorrow's opening night electric fountain display. The park crews, including about 70 W.P.A. (Work Projects Administration) workers, had been working overtime to complete it in time for the convention.

"Come on, girls. Let's walk down to the Bandstand and listen to the concert," Mother said Sunday evening as she pulled a light cardigan over her house dress. "Maybe we can find your father at the rock garden."

John Phillip Sousa marches wafted musically through the park, and the green park benches were filled with spectators. Children ran through the viewing areas chasing each other, or marched in time to the music. Feet tapped while people brushed mosquitoes away with practiced nonchalance.

Spotting Claire Humpal, a friend of hers, Mother sat down on one of the slatted benches to listen and visit. Carol and I stayed close to her for a time and watched enviously as other children scrambled after each other in the late twighlight hour.

After standing around for awhile to watch and listen as Vernon Malone directed the Virginia City Band, Carol and I inched slowly toward a group of children playing hide-and-seek among the deepening shadows of the fir trees. We still missed our old neighborhood and the early evening camaraderie of playing tin can tag on First Street North. Perhaps, some of the children playing were friends from Washington School where classes would begin again in two weeks.

I bent over to tie my shoelace when suddenly, someone grabbed and pulled me away from the pavilion, west toward the cemetery.

Thinking the tall boy was inviting me to play the game with the children, I ran after him, his hand grasping mine tightly as he pulled me along. Carol followed for a short distance, but not wanting to venture any further into the shadowed, ebbing light and away from the bandstand, she ran back to where Mother was sitting and sat down to examine a captured firefly.

When the march ended, Mother looked around and asked, "Where did your sister go? She was just here."

*Growing Up In Olcott Park* 45

"She's playing hide-and-go seek with those kids over there. She didn't ask me to play, either," Carol sighed. She had just turned seven and was used to being left behind when I played with my friends. Mother glanced toward the children who were hiding in shadows and behind trees. When it was safe to yell "free," they raced toward the designated home tree, trying to get there before "it" did. Thinking she'd spotted me and my blonde hair hiding in a nearby clump of bushes, she turned back to her friend, and continued to listen to the band play its concluding number. The final applause ended. People got up from their benches, said their goodbyes, and headed for their cars parked along the lower and center roads. They called to their children to join them.

The tall boy had pulled me toward a group of bushes near the bear den. I crouched down innocently, thinking we were hiding from the other children. His hands pushed me to lie down on the ground. I could see no other children and began to feel very uncomfortable as the boy started to grope at my blouse and sweater. I wasn't sure what was happening, but I knew this was no game. My happiness at being included quickly turned to terror.

A little over a year before, much news coverage was given to the execution of Bruno Hauptmann for the kidnapping and murder of Charles and Ann Morrow Lindbergh's 20-month old son. I was sure I was being kidnapped, and I began to wriggle and kick in an attempt to get away from the boy. He started to kiss my face and neck. I breathed in deeply to squelch a sob and to scream for Daddy to come and help me.

Anticipating my reaction, the boy put one hand over my mouth and said softly, "Don't make any noise, and I'll let you go."

Feeling his grubby hand on my mouth, I bit down on the skin of his palm as hard as I could. He jerked his hand away and at the same time, I pushed to my feet and ran toward the bandstand. In the distance, I could see people walking toward me on their way to their cars parked on the lower road near the animal pens. I looked back over my shoulder as I neared the first group, but didn't see the boy who had slipped into the shadows near the hedges lining the road.

My heart was racing when I spotted Mother and Carol who were searching for me in the thinning crowd.

"Ardys, you shouldn't run off like that," Mother scolded. "I was getting worried about you. It's almost dark. Come on, let's find your father."

Carol eyed me questioningly, but I took Mother's hand without a word, and we walked across the road toward the rock garden.

New walks and steps of granite flagstone led through the semi-formal, terraced gardens. A rectangular wall constructed of ornamental stone surrounded the lower pool area in whose center was the hexagonal, stone, electric fountain. The border and bank around the fountain section had been planted in evergreen trees and shrubs.

We found Daddy standing on the stone terrace talking to the crew of WPA workers who had been working overtime to complete the project. He invited them to stay for awhile longer, until the park closed and the concert-goers left, for a trial run of the fountain. A feeling of heady excitement was in the air as everyone waited.

Midsummer evenings in Northern Minnesota are long. Dusk creeps slowly toward darkness. By mid-August, the sun begins to meet the horizon of pine trees earlier, and a damp chill rises from lawns and lakes in the evening to give warning of Fall's imminent approach.

*Growing Up In Olcott Park*

We watched as the concert-goers gathered up their belongings and hurried toward their cars and warmer homes, drawing jackets and sweaters around themselves and their children as they left. Soon, the park had emptied and the big, iron entrance gates were closed.

We stood waiting on the stone terrace whose walls were constructed of native cut granite and greenstone coping when the fountain's switch was thrown. Water surged up from the center. Colored lights played on dancing streams of water that reached toward the sky; sometimes high, sometimes low; sometimes wide, sometimes narrow. Red, green, blue, yellow, in complimentary combinations.

We oohed and ahed and clapped our hands. The display was spectacular. The falling drops hit the water in the surrounding 45 by 60 foot square pool like a gentle rain and were recirculated to appear again in another form and color. It was even lovelier than the annual Fourth of July fireworks. The sounds of the falling water soothed and quieted, and none of us there had ever seen anything like it. None of us would ever forget it.

Daddy let it play for awhile, watching with satisfaction and listening to the favorable comments. It was a memorable evening for all who had been working on the rock garden and fountain for the past two years. Over 100 Virginians had developed it from piles of dirt and rock and created something beautiful that would be very special to all the people who lived on the Mesabi Iron Range far into the future.

"Well, Virginia is in for a treat tomorrow night," Daddy commented, as the fountain was turned off. "See you all in the morning. Thanks again for your hard work." Many of the men came over to shake his hand and congratulate him on the successful completion of the beautiful rock garden and fountain. Their sense of pride was obvious and well-earned.

Mother, Daddy, Carol and I walked back through the dark park toward the house. I held Mother's hand while Carol hung onto Daddy's arm. The greenhouse was dark; the bandstand was empty. The moon was playing its own game of hide-and-seek as it moved across the now cloudy sky.

I was quiet. My instincts told me not to spoil the magic of the evening by mentioning what had happened to me. Perhaps I had imagined it. Shirley Temple and Jane Withers would never have allowed any boy to drag them into the bushes. I bet the boy was just helping me to hide from the other children, and we hadn't been found. How could I tell anyone about what happened, because nothing really did happen. I was scared over nothing.

How embarrassing it would be to tell anyone. Daddy and Mother would be angry at me for running off like that in the dark. It was all my fault.

Silent alongside Mother, I was startled from my thoughts when I heard her call to Daddy and Carol who had run ahead, "Carl, let's go downtown and celebrate the fountain's completion. It's early, and Canelakes is still open."

"Good idea, Ink. Get in the car, girls, and start thinking about that rootbeer float."

It wasn't hard to do. Soon, my scary adventure in the bushes had been pushed by self-preservation to that place in my subconscious where scary things are denied, stored and covered up. I never told anyone about it. Even Carol. I never played hide-and-seek again, either.

### ADVICE

Young woman, beware—for your own sake
Of the "Guy" that's known as a "Common Rake."
Nor will he hesitate to deceive,
As his ancestor did with Mother Eve.
Young ladies, you shouldn't go strolling about
When your darling old mammas don't know you are out,
So remember, 'tis better be sure than be sorry.'
Then do not go strolling with Tom, Dick, or Harry.

J. H. Fleming, First Park Superintendent

# A PEEK INTO HISTORY

### Superintendents' Reports to Park Commission

*1923*
*"Greenhouse acquisition. 18' x 50' under glass."*

*April 1, 1933.*
*"The new Greenhouse built by the Virginia Park Commission during the fiscal year 1932-33 was designed and manufactured by Foley Greenhouse Manufacturing Company, Forest Park, Illinois.*
*"The building consists of one full iron frame flat rafte growing house. 50' wide x 92'3/4" long and vestibule entrance 11'3/4" wide x 5'10" deep. Glass from local companies. Cost: $2,897.67."*

*November, 1933*

"Open House Day—hundreds of visitors visited new greenhouse, this being the first chrysanthemum show ever sponsored in Virginia.

"The visitors were treated with an exhibition of hundreds of various types, sizes and blooms of chrysanthemums in many different colors and varieties, creating a most favorable impression.

"9 cement walks throughout the various aisles of the Greenhouse. Large palms grace center places, ferns scattered; baskets hanging, flowerpots. In winter 12,000 plants in view. In summer, 40,0000."

*1935*

"New greenhouse completed. Curtains on southside of roof, to save plants from direct rays of the real hot son. Kalsomine protected others."

*March, 1936*

"Band Concerts held at the parks, alternately on Sunday and Wednesday nights, are still proving a source of fine entertainment for Virginians, as well as many from nearby communities. The attendance has made it necessary to hold all Sunday night concerts at Olcott Park, and those on Wednesday night at the South Park."

"The Electric Fountain and Rock Garden now under construction will add a great deal to this widespread interest (in the park) because, it is the last word in modern park displays and will be one of the very few of its kind being developed in the United States."

"The thought that is paramount in the minds of the commissioners and park superintendent, is to cooperate at all times in the handling of the unemployment situation. During the past year we have had 15 regular employees and 70 part-time employees on our park payroll."
"WPA Projects were put through enabling the Park to secure more than 70% of federal money to assist in the project. $36,005.00 on Rock Garden, a 2-year project."
"Between the different ledges of rock, trees, and shrubbery, various types of rock garden plants will be planted. The Garden itself will be a sort of semi-formal affair, and at the present time, workmen are engaged hauling in suitable dirt for the legs. Flower beds arranged in terraces and outlined in Tufa rock or stone, will contain thousands of small rock garden plants of many different varieties. These plants are now being tried out in trial gardens and those found hardy enough for our severe winter climate will be utilized in this Rock Garden."

March, 1937
"The fountain is a G.E. Seven Projector Electric Fountain. Some 360 variations per hour are made possible with this combination of colored floodlights and several different sprays, all controlled automatically by rotary switches and an electric motor in the base of the fountain. Rock Garden plants and perennials being grown in the trial garden, will be planted in the slopes of the Pool Section. The area around the Fountain Section has been planted in evergreen trees and shrubs. Completed Rock Garden will cover about three acres. The fountain will run from 8:30 to 10:00 p.m. in summer."

March, 1937
"The Chrysanthemum Show held between November 5 and 15, drew 4,000 people. There were 2,500 plants displayed."

March, 1938
"Monday evening, August 16, 1937 the Fountain was turned on. It was necessary to have traffic policemen on the site to control the traffic. Interest continued until pool was drained in the Fall."

March, 1938
"140 part-time employees, 8 full-time employees."
"School Superintendent Levine instructed all grade teachers to visit the show with their classes. The children were instructed to tell their parents about the Mums and have them visit the show."

March, 1939
"Veterans of Foreign War Convention held July 5-6-7-8. (1938). Park employees worked from 4:00 a.m. to 1:00 p.m. so that our work would not interfere with convention activities. Governor Stassen spoke at the Memorial Service in Southside Park."

"The Fountain was in operation each night with the exception of a few nights when the wind was too strong. The Fountain Pool was drained,q cleaned and refilled. Water bugs have plugged the jets. We placed a number of suckers in the pool to clean out insects. Electric bill was $4.70."

July, 1941
"Foundations poured for the entrance gate. LaPatka has been cutting rock to match the old rock work."

*Fountain in Olcott Park*

*Carol and Ardys in front of fountain.*
*1942*

*View of Rock Garden and Fountain from park flagpole.*
*1941*

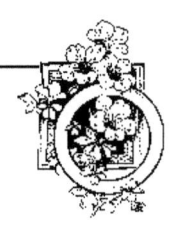

# THE VISITORS

In the summer of 1940, approximately fifty long-tailed, Ringtail Spider and Rhesus monkeys were residents of the impressive cement Monkey Island and drew visitors to the park from all over Northern Minnesota. Their antics were amusing and, in many instances, mirrored those of the spectators. The monkeys, native to tropical climates, appeared to enjoy their northern summer visit and were interesting in their novelty.

My sister and I gave a few of the more identifiable monkeys names like "Spider," "Sad Eyes," "Swingy" and "Little Babe" and often, early in the morning, we joined Frank to feed them bananas, apples, peanuts and lettuce. When he cleaned the island, we watched as he put on his high boots and lowered himself down a ladder into the watery moat that surrounded the castle-like structure. His long, high-powered hose washed peanut shells and melon rinds into piles, which he would sweep into a pail. We were not allowed to join him, but we watched from inside the fence around the cement wall and listened to the monkeys nervously screeching at Frank. Some monkeys lay in the sun on the island grooming each other, and others chased and swung by their tails from the rope ladder that was strung between two ash trees that grew on either side of the castle. People liked to watch the buffalo, elk, deer and bear; but the monkeys were the hands-down favorite of the zoo.

In September, with rising transportation costs and a poor exchange rate for returning the monkeys to the wholesaler, it was decided it would be cost effective to keep them through the winter. My father and Frank were very worried about the monkeys' welfare and their ability to withstand the frigid temperatures expected in our winters, but they decided it was worth the risk. The monkeys would winter in Minnesota.

The green "monkey house," as it was called when it was built in 1925, now held squirrels, beaver, guinea pigs and a wounded red fox, brought in by a forest ranger to recuperate. A new monkey cage, 6' by 22' 6", had been constructed on the second floor of the large utility garage next to the greenhouse. A circulating heater was purchased and promised to sufficiently heat the second-story where the monkeys would stay through the cold winter.

When the leaves began to fall and the nights turned chilly, the squawking monkeys were rounded up with a large net, transported to their new quarters, and put in the large cage where they swung about, did their grooming in small groups that huddled together, and watched for Frank, who brought their food. It wasn't Florida, but it would do. One December afternoon before Christmas, Carol met the bus that brought me from Junior High School, and we trudged home through the park from the Washington School. It had been snowing all day, and the branches of the tall pine trees were laden with heavy snow and hung like resplendent monarchs dressed in glistening finery. The road into the park had not been plowed yet, and we followed a pair of lonesome truck tracks leading through the silent drifts. We hurried, ignoring the squirrel and rabbit tracks in the fresh snow, and looked forward with great anticipation to seeing the four-legged visitors who had moved into our house that morning.

"I've been worrying about them all day, Ardys. That's why my push-pulls weren't slanted right and I didn't get a new pencil from Miss Prusha," Carol said. Miss Prusha was the school district Palmer Method Penmanship Teacher who scared the liver out of anyone who couldn't make properly slanted push-pulls and uniform circles. Handwriting wasn't Carol's strong suit.

"Mother said they'd get better. They just have bad colds. Come on, let's run," I replied, with concern in my voice. My handwriting hadn't been too great, either. Carol's lunch pail, emptied of its thermos of hot tomato soup, still smelled of her peanut butter and jelly sandwich and rattled at her side as we crunched toward home. Old enough now to eat in the cafeteria at the Junior High School, I had enjoyed a chopped ham and pickle sandwich, which I bought every day for twelve cents.

Our lined, rubber boots and heavy clothes protected us from the cold, north wind that had been blowing for almost a week. I wore prickly, woolen snowpants and a long, plaid jacket that looked like a blanket. A paisley square of wool covered most of my head. Carol wore a dark green, zippered, one-piece snowsuit and a matching helmet-like hat. To keep our hands warm, we wore heavy, home knit wool mittens, connected by crotcheted cords Mother had strung through our sleeves. The biting cold of the gray afternoon nipped at our noses and caused our breath to swirl away like clouds of smoke as we ran toward home. We raced up the back steps and into the entrance porch where we took off our boots and hung our outer gear on wall hooks near the basement steps.

"Yuk, it stinks in here," cried Carol, as she opened the kitchen door. On the stove was a large pot of steaming water into which Mother had spooned globs of camphored Vicks Vaporub. The house reeked with a strange mixture of smells and felt like a steamy sauna.

Every radiator in it knocked and hissed and radiated excessive amounts of heat.

Mother was talking on the big, black telephone that had its place in the alcove built into the wall of the dining room. She was holding a small animal in her arms and talking to Dr. Neff, who was giving her medical advice. Frank had been unable to locate the veterinarian, and Mother needed help.

"So you think it's pneumonia, Doctor? Is there something I can give them? Yes, they seem very feverish, and I am trying to get water down. Yes, I will call you again if I have to. Aspirin, too? How much? You're kidding! Well, thanks so much. Goodbye."

Hanging up the phone, she pushed back a lock of her dark brown hair and said, "If Dr. Neff is as good a doctor as your Dad says he is, he certainly should know what to do about our sick little monkeys."

"Look, Coo. Look at the monkeys. Oh, you poor babies," I cried, spotting the visitors and running around the table to the other end of the dining room.

Against the wall and under the windows, were three wire cages, each containing two lethargic monkeys wrapped in terry towels and torn flannel sheets. Their long tails lay uncovered and quivered weakly. Two large cartons next to the cages held four more very sick monkeys who lay bleating in piteous discomfort. Their eyes were clouded, with mucous discharge seeping from the corners. Instead of their usual raucous chatter, they wheezed, coughed and whimpered in an almost human manner.

Mother handed the swaddled monkey she was carrying to Carol who exclaimed, "It looks like Spider, Mother. Oh, no, not Spider. Please don't let him die."

She sat down on the davenport in the living room with the black, long-tailed spider monkey and rocked the sick little creature in her arms. She held it close until it fell asleep. She then laid it in an additional box that Mother had padded with newspapers. Carol's tears splashed on the monkey as she gently stroked its head.

We knew the monkeys were very sick because they would never let us touch them when they were well. Spider never did wake up. He and his box were gone in the morning.

"I don't want to go to school, Mother," cried Carol the next day when she awoke to the news that Spider had died.

"Carol, you can help me nurse the other monkeys when you get home," promised Mother, as she braided my hair into pigtails. "Spider was very sick, and we tried the best we could to make him well. Go and get dressed now. It's getting late."

We nursed the monkeys for four days in the hot Olcott Park house. Outside, the daytime temperatures persisted at below-zero. Mother slept on the davenport in the living room so she could keep the sick, tropical creatures covered and warm at night. She continued to urge them to drink water, rubbed their furry chests with camphored grease, and laughingly complained, "I think I know how Mrs. Dionne feels with five babies." (The Dionne quintuplets had been born in Canada two years before, and pictures of the cute little girls were still featured in every magazine and newsreel.) As the days passed, two more monkeys joined the dining room nursery to replace the few that died, but little by little, the monkeys gained strength and began to drink their water and occasionally eat a little bite of banana. I thought of suggesting cod-liver-oil, but thought that would make them even sicker. They now huddled together, instead of lying wrapped in blankets, and we couldn't hold them anymore.

Finally Daddy said, "We've sealed the windows of the garage, and it has warmed up a little, so I think we can get these smelly animals out of here today." By this time, the remaining monkeys were doing much better.

"Ink," he said to my Mother, "you and your two tow-headed nurses have saved over half the sick monkeys. You can take care of me anytime." He kissed Mother, whose name was Inga but was called Inky by her friends, and Carol and I reached up for one, too. He went out the back door to tell Frank to come and pick up his monkeys.

Mother answered a knock at the back door one day soon after the monkeys moved out. Frank stood there with a huge bouquet of yellow and maroon chrysanthemums in his arms. After scraping the snow from his boots, he shyly stepped into the kitchen and said, "The monkeys sent these down to you. They all say thanks and Merry Christmas." He sat down to enjoy a cup of coffee with Mother and give her an update on the monkeys' health.

No one was sorry to see those monkeys return to their winter home above the garage. It was Spring before the combination of monkey odor and camphor left our house. Mother burned incense and sprayed cologne on the rugs. Even on sunny days, it was still too cold to open the windows to air the house. Eventually, everything had to be cleaned, aired and deodorized, as even freshly baked ginger cookies and Christmas Eve lutefisk failed to mask the pungent monkey odor.

After that, the Olcott Park monkeys always flew South to spend the winter.

## A PEEK INTO HISTORY

### Superintendents' Reports to Park Commission

*March, 1916*
*"Monkeys are a source of constant amusement, and it is recommended that a male Ringtail be secured as a mate for the female we now have, and also a pair of Spider Monkeys be secured.*

*Growing Up In Olcott Park*

*This latter variety is the most active one for park purposes and area and a source of constant amusement for the spectators."*

March 1935
*"Hundreds yet thousands of visitors come to our Olcott Park for a view of the monkeys and their larger antics have thrilled both old and young. Many visitors from out-of-town places make it a point to visit the so-called Monkey Island."*

March 31, 1938
*"A new monkey cage was constructed on the second floor of the garage, size 6' by 22'6". Circulating heater installed. Ceiling insulated."*

August 30, 1940
(Regarding the International Truck purchased in 1930)
*"750 gallon water tank was mounted on the truck chassis and the new pumping unit installed. This unit operated even better than we expected. A very high pressure can be produced, with plenty of volume. It worked very well, washing out the Monkey Island pool."*

September 31, 1940
*"The International pumper was used to flush out the Monkey Island twice each week, to wash out the bear dens, water the deer pasture, flush out the sewers and drainage lines. All catch basin sumps were cleaned out. Excavation completed for sewer manhole, south of the garage."*

November, 1940
*"Zoo—One white deer fawn and one red deer fawn were killed by the bucks this month. This happens when the deer get in close quarters inside the shelters."*

*January 31, 1941*

*"The monkeys are in first class shape and seem to be doing well. This is gratifying in view of the fact that the present quotation on Rhesus Monkeys is $15.00 each and they are hard to get."*

*March 31, 1941*

*"The cost of feeding animals was less even though we had more heavy feeders such as elk, deer and buffalo; and kept our monkeys over the winter."*

*May 31, 1941*

*"Fifty monkeys were ordered from Henry Trefflich to be held for the account of the National Foundation for Infantile Paralysis, Inc. The Park Department to pay for express from New York and to the destination as they are ordered out. The Monkey Island was cleaned and sealed. Monkeys placed on the Island on May 31st."*

*July 31, 1941*

*"Very warm weather. Inventory of animals: 45 Monkeys, 12 Elk, 4 Native Deer, 3 Black Fallow Deer, 10 White Fallow Deer, 4 Bear, 4 Buffalo. We also have scads of rabbits, too numerous to mention."*

*September 31, 1941*

*"The balance of the monkeys were shipped to the Infantile Paralysis Foundation. The Monkey Island was cleaned and drained for the winter."*

*June 30, 1942*

*"50 monkeys received by express on June 4th. Three had colds when received. One was in tough shape. All monkeys were placed*

*in the animal house. The first 10 days in June were very cold and wet. The monkeys were placed on the Island on June 12th. From June 1st to the 30th there were just four nights when the temperature was above 50. We lost six monkeys on the Island."*

*October 31, 1942*
*"The monkeys were crated and shipped back to Trefflich on October 6th."*

*February 28, 1943*
*"Two large dogs got down in the Monkey Island and killed six rabbits. We still have 16 left. We had placed wooden rearing boxes in the Island the week before, and the 16 rabbits that came through took refuge in the boxes. The dogs were disposed of."*

*July, 1951*
*"The monkey that escaped the island returned after ten days."*

*July 31, 1956*
*"We lost over half our monkeys due to cold nights below 50. Every few days we lose a monkey. Saw Dr. Nankervis today, and he advised giving them sulfa in water. This proved to be quite a project. Water was withheld and during the night monkeys would lap up moisture on concrete from dew or rain and then refused to drink the water with sulfa."*

*May 30, 1964*
*"Ordered 15 rhesus monkeys from Henry Trifflich Co. Monkeys arrived on June 4th. Vandals started killing monkeys as soon as they were put on the island. We decided not to have monkeys next year."*

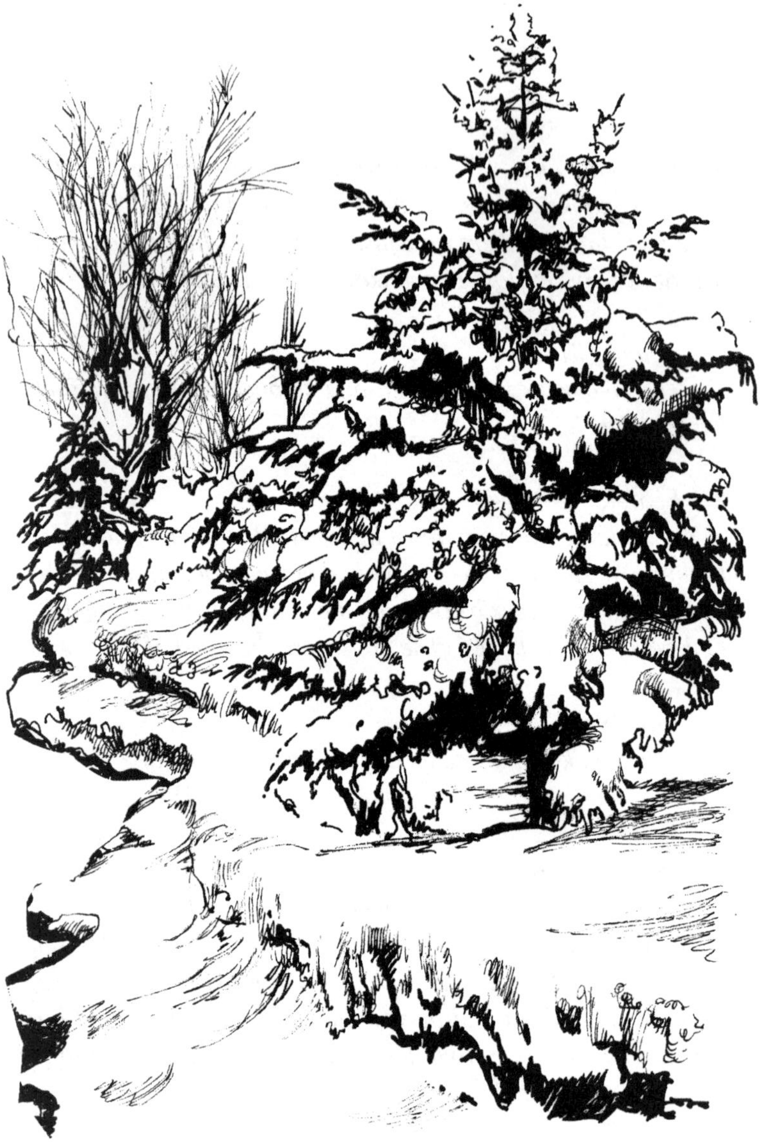

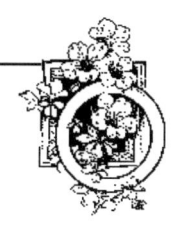

# CREEP ACROSS THE TRESTLE

It was Saturday. Carol and I were walking home after spending the afternoon at the Granada Theater with our movie serial hero of the month, Hopalong Cassidy. We usually went the back way, along the railroad track that ran parallel to the lake, where we picked up coal chunks dropped from the coal tenders feeding the steam engines that used the tracks. Feeling especially brave that day, I decided we would shortcut and walk across the trestle spanning the northeast end of Silver Lake. The D.W. & P. evening train was guaranteed to arrive at exactly 10:10 p.m., about six hours away. We had enviously watched other kids crossing the trestle, but always chickened out whenever we considered doing it ourselves.

Empowered by the brave Hopalong, I called, "Come on, Carol. I'm going to walk the trestle." Carol balked.

"Come on. Don't be such a sissy," I taunted, as I clambered up the small hill near the west end of First Street North that led to the tracks.

The trestle was wooden and had two small platforms extending from its sides, each about a third of the way from either end. Daddy told us the platforms were there so anyone working on the trestle would have a place to stand if a train came.

The ties were slippery that day. The space between them seemed wide enough for a foot to easily slip through. I could see the frozen lake below, and it looked like a long way down.

Maybe we shouldn't do this, I reasoned to myself, beginning to have second thoughts.

By this time, Carol had climbed up and was carefully stepping on the ties behind me. "I don't think we should do this, Ardys," she said. "Mother will get mad at us if she finds out."

"Don't you dare tell her or anybody," I threatened. "We're this far; we might as well go the rest of the way."

At nine years old, Carol lived by the rules; black was black, and white was white. Nothing in-between. From my jaded, older sister perspective, she was also a tattle-tale. I spent many hours doing time in my room because of her forthright honesty.

I carefully put one foot ahead of the other until I reached the first platform where I waited for her. It was cold, and now that we had no buildings or trees to protect us, we could feel the wind blow freely over the lake. Swirls of snow blew up and onto our faces.

"It sure is a long way down there," Carol commented, as she cautiously peered over the railing of the first platform to the lake below, about eight feet away. "Let's keep going. I'm getting cold."

We pulled up the collars of our wool jackets and set off again toward the center of the trestle. The ties were closer together than our normal walking steps. We had to watch carefully so we wouldn't miss one and slip through. It was very slow. Turning back was no longer an option. Turning around was too scary to consider.

"Ding Clack Ding Clack." Hearing the signal bell behind me, and with dread in my heart, I took a quick look over my shoulder. A chill, colder than any I had felt earlier on the platform, grabbed my stomach and put it in my mouth.

"Oh, Ardys," cried Carol. "Here comes a train. Oh, no. What should we do?"

I reached back and grabbed her mittened hand and pulled her up to me.

"It isn't a train," I said. "It's only a handcart." I didn't want her to start crying in the middle of the trestle.

"What difference does that make? It's still coming," she logically argued. Two railroad workers faced each other and vigorously pumped the handles of the handcart. They were getting closer. One had his back to us, and the other had his face down to protect him from the wind. They didn't see us.

"Come on, Coo. We've just got to move faster," I scolded, as I pulled her along. We had already passed the middle of the trestle where it began its curve toward the north bank of the lake. The wind off the frozen lake was raw, and the ties seemed icier. I held tightly to Coo's hand, and we gingerly inched our way toward the second platform. Behind us, we could hear the handcart gaining on us.

"Why don't we crawl, Ardys? That will be easier," Carol suggested. "It's a shorter distance to the lake if we slip, too." We both bent over, got down on our hands and knees, and like two crabs, started our creep toward safety.

"Ho there," we heard behind us. "What have we here?"

"Looks like it might be a couple of bear, Joe. Should we shoot 'em?"

The pumping stopped. The handcart was right behind us. Two men, dressed in heavy jackets, overalls, woolen caps, and gloves, were standing on the cart enjoying the scene in front of them. Carol and I continued our embarrassing crawl to the platform, which was now only a few feet away.

"Well, what do you know. They aren't bear, after all. Sure glad we didn't shoot 'em," said Joe. They slowly pumped the cart to keep up with us. "Want a ride, girls?"

It was tempting. But, we had been warned to never accept rides from strangers.

A few more crawls, and we reached the platform.

"Come on, girls. Hop on and we'll give you a ride to the end. You shouldn't be out here like this."

We still had one-third of the way to creep across the cold, icy trestle. I looked at Carol standing on the platform, her teeth chattering from both fright and cold, and rationalized aloud, "Well, nobody told us to not accept a ride on a stranger's handcart."

We clambered aboard, embarrassed and grateful. The cart was slowly pumped to the edge of the lake where we could jump to safety. The men waved and yelled, "Hey, you kids better stay off this trestle 'cause next time you might get shot." We heard them laughing as they pumped off down the track.

That was the only time either of us crept across the trestle. For once, Carol believed my threat of "silence, or else." It was years later, when we were all old enough to get a good laugh over it, that we told Mother, who humorously agreed that it was probably a good idea to have accepted that ride on the D. W. & P. handcart. "It was probably safer than a lot of those cars you rode off in when you were in high school."

True.

# A PEEK INTO HISTORY

## Superintendent's Report to Park Commission

*March 31, 1919*
*"Recreation is necessary in one form or another for everybody, but particularly, for children.*

*The playground is a form of social insurance, and the movements for playground work has become an established part of all city life, where forms of both physical and mental enjoyment can be indulged in by the children, the same being conducted under proper supervision and instruction, during the time the public schools are closed."*

*March 31, 1932*
*"The games of children can be used not only to enlarge their lungs and straighten their backs, but also as character building for civic and social virtues. Children learn to wait their turn, to be fair and honest, to lose with good humor and to care more for the game than the prize."*

*Municipal Bathing Beach,
Virginia, Minnesota*

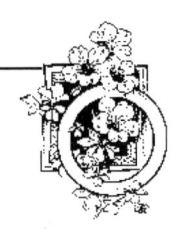

## THE TWINS

One Saturday morning in early Spring of 1942, Daddy honked from his truck, which was parked with its engine running on the cinder road outside the back door of the house. Carol and I ran out to see what was going on. He was grinning from ear to ear and said, "Get in, I've got something to show you."

A rare trip in Daddy's truck always promised something special. I excitedly jumped up on the high, black leather seat beside him and pulled Carol in after me. We drove to the far west end of the park, stopping on the road next to the elk pasture. Daddy reached to the ledge in back of the cab of the pickup and brought out two leather leashes and two small dog collars.

"Oh, Daddy, did you get us a dog?" cried Carol. Almost beside herself, she scrambled down and fell in the gravel on the side of the road.

"Don't be such a dummy, Coo. You know there are no dogs allowed in the park," I said, quite sanctimoniously, as I watched her brush the dirt off her jodphurs.

"Dogs can't read, Ardys. How do they know?" pouted Carol, who had continued to beg for a dog long after she could read the "No Dogs Allowed" signs posted throughout the park.

"Come on, girls. I've got something even better than a dog," said Daddy. With one of us on hanging on each of his arms, he walked across the road toward a group of park employees gathered near the bear dens.

Frank was standing with two, fuzzy, black bear cubs in his arms. Armed with a long pole, he had borrowed them from their mother who was now locked in the cement den where she had been lured with food. The hungry, older bear, who had spent a long winter of fasting while in hibernation, didn't seem to be overly stressed to have Frank kidnap two of her cubs.

Frank attached the collars and leashes to the cubs' necks and suggested Carol and I take them for a walk through the park. He gave strict instructions to keep the bear away from small children and to follow their lead, so they wouldn't get too tired.

Overjoyed, we petted the soft cubs who crawled up our backs, sucked our fingers, and licked our faces with their wet, sandpaper-like tongues. Finally, with leashes secure and safety reminders repeated, the four of us ran off.

"Oh, they're so cute and soft," exclaimed Carol. "They're like roly poly balls of fur. They look like little puppies."

"Yes, they're cute, but they smell so bad," I countered, and ran after her.

The twins had spent their first six weeks in the den with their mother and carried her very strong odor. When we petted the animals, the oil from their fur caused our hands to smell the same way.

Remembering Frank's cautions, we guided the bear toward home to show them to Mother, stopping every once in awhile to pick them up and nuzzle their furry bodies. They stopped to sniff at a few trees and bushes on the way, but they hadn't learned yet that they were climbers. When we reached the house, Mother was expecting us and came outside to admire the cubs. Wisely, after smelling the four of us, she refused to allow any of us inside.

Until they got too big to be safe playmates, Carol, the bear cubs, and I spent many hours playing on the lawn in front of the house. The bear cubs had been separated from their mother and now lived in the monkey cage above the garage. We fed them milk from baby bottles and named them "Roly" and "Poly." We learned to tell them apart by the coloring of their noses.

Visitors to the park took pictures and laughed delightedly as the bear climbed and frolicked with us. Most of them didn't want to pet the animals or get too close because, by this time, even after the several baths Frank helped us give them, the bear-grease odor emanating from all four of us was still very strong. After we fed the bear their bottles in the early morning, they poked and tumbled, chased each other and climbed on us as we lay on our backs in the grass.

"Stop that!" I screamed one day, pulling Roly away from my head. "He chewed my pigtail," I wailed. Sure enough, the bear was mouthing one of the rubber bands that had fastened the end of my braid. One skinny, blonde pigtail was slimy wet and definitely shorter than the other. A tell-tale strand of my hair hung limply from the corner of his mouth.

The next time we begged Frank to let us take the cubs for a walk he said, "No, it's not safe for you to take them out anymore, girls. The twins are getting big enough to live outside now. We're going to put them in the den next to Mama and Papa Bear."

That was a sad day for Carol and me, as we could only visit our little friends from a distance, outside the fence of their den. Several days later, Daddy sat in the big chair by the front window reading the <u>Virginia Daily Enterprise</u> when Carol and I ran through the front door. It was time for Jack Armstrong, the All American Boy , and we wanted to find out if Jack had rescued his dog from the raging waters. We turned on the radio and sat in front of it on the oriental carpet in the living room.

Daddy lowered his paper and said to Mother, who was sitting on the davenport knitting, "Boy, it smells good in here. Are you wearing some new kind of perfume?"

I caught his wink and looked back at Mother who responded, "No, I'm not wearing any perfume. I think that nice smell is called Essence of Young Girls."

"Well, it sure beats that Eu d'pu that we've had around here lately. I even have an appetite again."

To the west, in the crowded coziness of the double-sided bear den, Mama and Papa Bear were probably gruffing their version of the same comment.

# A PEEK INTO HISTORY

### Superintendents' Reports to Park Commission

*April 19, 1915*
*"New den for the bear completed."*

*March 30, 1930*
*"No Dogs Allowed apparently has no meaning to many dog owners and their children when visiting the park. A growing menace to the Zoo which is inviting the question as the reasonableness of either doing away with the deer and elk or persuing a more forcible policy to prevent the animals being chased by dogs."*

# The Twins

*March 31, 1937*
"A great improvement was made in the bear dens when the concrete floor was removed and replaced with peat and sand. This eliminates to a great extent, the danger of the bear contracting pneumonia."

*December, 1940*
"The bears came out of their dens during the mild weather, just before Christmas. All animals are in good shape."

*January 31, 1942*
"Judging from the sounds heard in the bear den, at least one cub was born in January."

*February 28, 1942*
"The cub bears are still alive and are now about five weeks old. As soon as it is safe to do so, we will remove the cubs from the den."

*March 31, 1942*
"We found that three cubs were born to one of the bears. When the cubs were about 7 weeks old, two were removed from the den and put in the animal cage above the garage. The other cub was left with the mother. The cubs are doing very well."

*May 30, 1942*
"One bear cub lost."

*October , 1942*
"Four bear disposed of by State Game Wardens."

*March, 1943*
*"There were indications that we had some new bear cubs the first week in March, but we could not hear them after that. It is impossible to raise cubs with two females in one den."*

*Roly and Poly on front steps of
Olcott Park House*

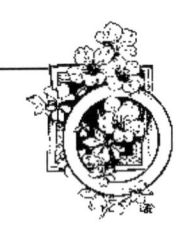

## BUSTER

Every summer, Carol and I spent two weeks with our Grandma and Grandpa Teigen on a small farm near Wrenshall, about seventy miles south of Virginia. Grandpa farmed alfalfa, cabbages, potatoes, rutabagas, raspberries, and always had a full coop of chickens. Each Spring he bought two baby pigs, which he fed well and named Carol and Ardys. In the Fall, he slaughtered and hung the meat in the smokehouse with the venison, partridge, duck and pheasants he, Daddy, and my uncles hunted. He milked four Jersey cows. Two very large dray horses pulled his plow and wagons.

The horses and cows pastured in a cleared field scattered with stumps, bright yellow buttercups, and several broken-down cars. On warm days, Grandma sometimes packed a jelly sandwich, an apple, and a big, round sugar cookie for each of us and sent Carol and me out to the pasture with an empty lard pail to pick cherries. When we tired of picking the chokecherries and pincherries growing on bushes along the property fence at the back of the pasture, we climbed into the torn, black leather rumble seat of a Model A Ford, which was sitting in the pasture along with several other old wrecks.

We pretended we were going to California. Hollywood, California. We became Shirley Temple and Jane Withers riding west in the battered heap. When this bored us, we pushed and teased Silver, the white dray horse, to the fence and climbed atop his back. Without reins or saddle, we sat on the large horse in our shirts and denim overalls and pretended we were cowgirls. The meadowlarks sang in the fields, and fluffy, white clouds moved lazily across the sky. The big horses pulled at blades of grass, while brushing flies with their tails. We moved slowly as Silver grazed, but in our imaginations, we were galloping after stagecoaches with Hopalong Cassidy and Wild Bill Hickock and sometimes, Roy Rogers, depending on which serial we'd seen most recently at the Granada Theater.

Occasionally, after using the gentle work horses to pull his plow or hay wagon, Grandpa would let us ride bareback up and down the two-rut field road leading to one of the farm's two root cellars. It was a far cry from the exciting rides the Hollywood cowgirls were enjoying but, for two little city girls from the Iron Range, it was great adventure. We loved the slow, friendly horses and helped our Grandfather brush and feed them when they returned to their stalls in the smelly old barn.

A special treat for us was when Grandpa lead the horses to be reshod at the blacksmith in the village, about a mile down the road. Watching their hooves being scraped and listening to the clanging hammering of the horseshoes fascinated us. We chomped on black licorice sticks Grandpa bought for us at the big, cluttered General Store and watched the blacksmith lift the horses' feet one-by-one to shod them with the iron horseshoes. The blacksmith always had a plug of snuff stuffed into the pouch of his cheek and spat in a pail, which stood in a corner on the straw-covered dirt floor of the large, open shop. Carol and I watched his technique closely. And later, after considerable practice, we learned how to spit black licorice a reasonably respectable distance.

"I love horses," I dreamily commented as the family returned home one Sunday evening, following Carol's and my two-week visit with our grandparents.

Carol hesitantly replied, "Me, too." Lying together in Grandma's double bed in the guest bedroom of the farmhouse the night before and looking at the plaque on the wall that said "Watch and Pray," Carol had confessed a fear to me. The horses seemed so big. She liked Grandma's dog Flip much better.

"I wish I had a horse. I'd keep him in the big field outside the fence at home and ride him every day." I closed my eyes and envisioned myself as a brave, Jane Withers-style cowgirl. I was daringly rescuing an entire pioneer family captured by fierce, painted Indians.

Carol usually agreed with me in matters of such importance, but she was quiet. Soon, we were both asleep in the huge backseat of the big, 1936 Franklin.

One day about a week later, Mother said, "Girls, go and wash up. We're all going in the car to a farm just south of Eveleth to see some animals. Be sure you go to the bathroom before we leave."

When questioned about what animals we were going to see, Daddy said, "We're going to see a man about a dog," a favorite expression of his that I interpreted correctly as, either "I have to go to the bathroom" or "Don't ask any more questions. I'm not telling."

At mention of a dog, Carol's eyes lit up, and she nudged me, hopefully. The car was backed out of the garage and soon, the four of us were speeding at forty miles an hour down the short piece of iron highway south of Eveleth toward Duluth.

We passed two lakes and several stands of Norway Pine, and came to a road leading to a yellow farmhouse near a corral where several horses and ponies grazed. We turned onto the narrow road and stopped, the big tires of the Franklin kicking up gravel from the driveway. Pushing open the heavy back door of the car, Carol and I ran to the white corral to see the horses that were standing there. Mother followed us, while Daddy headed toward the farmhouse.

Pulling out two apples hidden in her large pocketbook, Mother gave one to each of us. Carol started to eat hers.

"That's not for you, Coo. Give it to that horse over there," I scolded, as I leaned over the fence toward a chestnut Welsh pony that had run to me when he saw the apple.

The pony was larger than a Shetland, but much smaller than Grandpa's drays. His mane was thick, and his nose pushed aggressively at me in search of a second apple. Long eyelashes framed big, brown eyes, and his full, blond tail swished and swept his backside. His strong, stocky legs explained why his ancestors had pulled heavy coal bins in Welsh mines. Daddy and the animal's owner soon joined us. "Would you like to ride the pony, girls?" he asked.

"Oh, yes, Daddy, yes!" I jumped up and down, pigtails bobbing on my shoulders. Coo was quiet. Looking nervously at the horse's huge teeth, prancing feet and swishing tail, she moved closer to Mother. She had almost finished the apple and now pulled at Mother's arm and asked to be taken to the bathroom. I heard her ask Mother if Daddy had talked to the man about the dog.

A bridle was placed over the horse's head, and a small saddle was strapped over a blanket on its back. I patted the horse and danced expectantly while everything was being secured. Soon, I was sitting in the saddle. The horse's owner was leading me around the corral. My afternoons with Hopalong at the Granada Theater had paid off. I sat tall in the saddle; my feet were firmly planted in the stirrups. It was glorious.

"He seems gentle enough," observed Mother. She had returned with Carol, who was standing close to her side. Mother's only experience with horses were Grandpa's big, slow moving drays. If she had only known.

"What do you think, Ardys? Can you handle him?" asked Daddy, knowing my reply.

"Oh, I love him, Daddy." I was handed the reins and obediently, the little horse walked in a circle around the corral. I could hardly believe this was happening. Under my breath, I exultantly exclaimed, "It's just like in the movies." I patted the Welsh's smooth neck, and he looked back at me with a gleam in one of his big, brown eyes. When offered a ride, Carol declined, although she let the horse lick her hand to finish off what remained of their apple.

Daddy bought the pony that day. Buster, the name already given the Welsh, was delivered to the park two days later. He moved into his tiny barn, an old shack of a building with a half-door located in back of the greenhouse near the three large compost piles. The shed had at one time sheltered a pair of buggyhorses. Old harnesses, reins and pieces of dusty horse blankets still hung on the wall. Accompanying Buster was a western saddle and bridle, a small sleigh, and a black surrey, pony-size.

Buster was mean. His good behavior vanished in his new surroundings. Carol rode him twice. After a terrifying ride and ditch-off onto the road, she refused to get on his back again. The younger men on the park crew rode him, trying to tame him a bit. Mother, the all-time monkey nurse and animal lover, still believing Buster was a gentle pony, rode him and was bucked off. Her foot caught in a stirrup, and Buster dragged her through the compost and cinders toward the barn. After an emergency visit to Dr. Neff, she was laid up for several weeks with two broken ribs.

I loved him. I visited the small barn every day to brush him, change his water, and feed him his hay and oats. Frank taught me how to saddle him. The park crew encouraged and gave me riding tips. I discovered that sugar lumps worked best as bribes, and they filled my jodhpur pockets until the day Buster ripped off one of the pockets with his sharp teeth to get at the treats inside. To supplement Hopalong's exampled riding, I borrowed a book at the Northside Library —"How to Ride and Care For a Horse."

Unfortunately, Buster couldn't read. He allowed me to ride him through the park, but he knew who was boss. Occasionally, to prove it, he would suddenly rear up, race toward the elk or buffalo pens and try to rub me off his back by hugging the chain link fence. Other times, after a reasonably pleasant ride, he would decide to go home. He put his head down and raced toward his barn and its low, dutch-door frame. If I left the bottom part of the door open, I had to put my face in the horse's mane so I wouldn't get my head knocked off going into the barn.

"You have to show him who's boss, Ardys. Be firm with him. You have to hold his reins tightly, and use your heels to guide him," said Daddy, who was angry at the horse and wondered why he had bought him. He was worried Buster would hurt me, even though I rode almost every day and claimed I wasn't afraid of him.

I was terrified. I thought I could make a friend of Buster. He didn't behave like the horses in the movies at all. I told Carol, who, again under threat, was sworn to secrecy about all the times Buster bucked and rubbed me off his back. I often had to chase him home after he deposited me in a bush somewhere in the park. Thankfully, my pride was bruised more often than my body.

One winter day after a fresh snowfall, Daddy gave into my pleas and requested that Frank hitch Buster to the small sleigh, which had not been used since its delivery. When Frank, Buster and the little sleigh arrived at the back door of the house, Carol, with some coaxing, and I were ready to go. We pulled on our mittens and climbed into the sleigh. I took the reins from Frank, half-listening to his few directions.

"Just like in the movies," I thought, confident I knew what I was doing. I had recently seen the movie *Heidi*, and in it, Shirley Temple had driven a similar sleigh. My brave heart was racing in anticipation of this new thrill. Traveling with Buster was always exciting and unpredictable.

Carol sat bravely beside me on the hard, wooden seat. I could tell she didn't know if she thought this was fun, or not. One thing I knew for sure, she didn't want me to call her a sissy as we had settled that on the railroad trestle a long time ago. She hung on to one side of the sleigh and waved at Mother, who stood in the snow wringing her hands and rubbing her back. "Don't go out of the gates, girls," she called after us.

In response, Buster put his head down and demurely trotted toward the park gates and Ninth Street. Suddenly, with a twitch of his ears and a swish of his tail, he dug his little hooves into the snow, went through the park gate, and quickly turned the corner. Tasting release and a bit of undiscovered land, he picked up speed and raced down the hill toward Sixth Avenue. Standing on the floor of the little sleigh, I pulled the reins as tightly as I could and yelled, "Whoa, Buster! Whoa!" at the top of my lungs. Not surprisingly, Buster paid no heed. Carol hung tightly onto the seat of the sleigh, closed her eyes and screamed, "Stop him, Ardys. I want to get off. I hate this ride!"

Buster was jubilant in his new freedom. His short legs pulled us downhill with seeming ease and increasing speed. The sleigh careened on the bumpy, snow-covered sidewalk. Several people driving past stopped their cars to watch as the small horse pulled us, terrorized, toward certain disaster. Carol started to cry and even I, the bravest cinema rider of all, had wet my pants and was scared to death.

When all seemed lost, Frank, in his little black pickup, raced like a shot out of the park and chased us down the hill. He passed the sleigh, drove over the curb and onto the sidewalk and stopped a short distance in front of the headstrong horse. I tugged hard at the reins, and Buster skidded to a stop before hitting the truck. Frank jumped out and grabbed his halter. Leaving his truck there, he led the exhilarated pony and the cowgirls, still scared and shaken, back to the barn.

Buster spent the following Spring and Summer loosely tethered in the empty field east of the park. He lived well. He was visited and petted by the Northside children who short-cut their way to downtown through the field and fed him smuggled apples and sugar lumps. I rode him occasionally, but almost overnight, this cowgirl had become Deanna Durbin, a movie soprano who did not ride horses.

Daddy wisely sold the pony to a family of three boys who lived on a farm north of town. On Buster's last day in the park, I fed him some extra oats and brushed his mane. With tears welling in my eyes at the loss of this one-sided friendship, I smelled his shiny coat, kissed his neck and said goodbye.

Later, as I watched Buster's three new boys dance excitedly around him while he was being loaded into their trailer, I remembered when I felt the same way.

One day a few weeks after the horse moved from the small barn, I unsuccessfully tried to hide a smile when Daddy told me that one of Buster's new boys broke his leg when thrown by the fiesty little Welsh.

Carol never again rode any horse; but she always owned a dog.

## THE ARAB'S FAREWELL TO HIS HORSE

My beautiful! my beautiful! that standest meekly by,
With thy proudly arch'd and glossy neck, and dark and fiery eye,
Fret not to roam the desert now, with all they winged speed;
I may not mount on thee again,—thour't sold, my Arab steed!
Fret not with that impatient hoof,—snuff not the breezy wind,—
The farthest that thou fliest now, so far am I behind:
The stranger hath thy bridle-rein,—
thy master hath his gold,—
Fleet-limb'd and beautiful, farewell; thou'rt sold, my steed, thou'rt sold.

Caroline Norton

## A PEEK INTO HISTORY

**Virginia Daily Enterprise**

*February 2, 1915*
" *Seventy-five buffalo at $300.00 each purchased by State for it's Parks—from Scotty Phillips buffalo herd at Ft. Pierre, Montana—1,000 animals being disposed of by Phillips estate administrator.*"

## Superintendents' Reports to Park Commission

*March 31, 1935*
"*The Buffalo are still a source of amusement to many visitors, for the slow, plodding, docile animals at times, show their fierceness.*
"*The Elk are always suspicious of visitors, and to protect the many who watch their antics, heavy fences have been put up.*
"*The Bear, as usual, pace back and forth in their cages.*"

*March 31, 1939*
"*Ford V-8 drove 585 miles, using 70.9 gallons gas and two quarts of oil. Average miles per gallon—8.2.*"

*March 31, 1941*
"*A new runway is going to be constucted below the animal enclosures which will permit us to shift the animals from one enclosure to another.*"

*December 31, 1941*
"*Two white deer delivered to the Zoo at Duluth. Three llamas brought back.*"

*March 31, 1942*
"*Nine loads of horse manure hauled from Hellman's pony farm for hot beds.*"

# THE WINTER FROLIC

I was ready for the race. The new, beige ice skates Mother and Daddy had given me for my eleventh birthday in January were polished and very sharp. I had really hoped for white figure skates like Sonja Henie's, but after skating around the ice rink at the Jefferson School a few times, I knew that, as usual, my Daddy knew best. I was fast.

It was Saturday, February 24, 1940, the official first day of the sixth annual St. Louis County Winter Frolic. Over 10,000 winter sports enthusiasts were expected to crowd Virginia's special frolic centers. There would be activities at the Memorial Recreation building, the Silver Lake Play Center, the Iron Bowl Winter Sports Center, Chestnut Street frolic areas, and the rural snow train headquarters at the Duluth, Mesabi and Iron Range railroad depot where, on Sunday, more than 900 people would swarm off a special 15-car snow train from Duluth and stations along the route of the Duluth Mesabe &Iron Range Railroad. A curling bonspiel, county hockey championship games, Girls' State High School Swim Meet, and two parades were scheduled.

The highlights of the two-day event were, in my estimation, the moonlight dedication tonight at the Iron Bowl, the large, winter sports area fashioned in Sliver Pit, an emptied iron ore mine on the north edge of town, and the skating races for my age group at Silver Lake. The second annual Virginia Ski Tournament would take place at the Iron Bowl Sunday afternoon where there would also be tobaggan races, slalom contests, and cross country ski marathons.

In basements and garages all across the county, skates of all sizes had been sharpened and skis waxed. Sub-zero weather failed to chill the enthusiasm of rural and city children who were scouting for large, slippery pieces of cardboard for the bump slides and tightening the weave on their snowshoes. Fifty-one special competitive events were planned, in addition to the coronation of Her Imperial Majesty, Miss Rural St. Louis County VI and Her Royal Highness, Miss Rural High School.

I looked at the clock on the kitchen wall as I choked down the tuna sandwich Mother forced me to eat. "It will help you skate faster, Ardys." I held my breath and took another bite, washing it down with a big glass of Bosco. Noone could skate any faster. I planned to win my race.

"Hurry, now. Daddy will be here in a few minutes to take you to Silver Lake for the Virginia children's races. He has to be at the Fay Hotel for the Frolic leadership luncheon. Be sure to go to the bathroom, and for luck, wear those new, blue mittens I knit for you."

Carol had a bad cold and was in bed. I ran up the stairs two at a time and peeked in her room. "Wish me luck, Coo. Wish you could come, too." I pushed the cords of the lucky mittens through the sleeves of my woolen jacket. "What a time to get sick."

"You'll win, Ardys," she said, in between sneezes. "Be sure you tie your skates so you don't trip." Carol was my number one booster.

Dressed in woolen snow pants and jacket, I waited anxiously at the back door for Daddy. He had been busy for weeks with the preparation of many of the various frolic areas and was especially proud of the Iron Bowl, which was in its second year of use and

## The Winter Frolic

under the supervision of the Park Department. "I hope he doesn't forget me," I thought. Hearing the car crunch over the snowy, cinder road, I tied my woolen cap under my chin and ran outside. Jumping into the car's warm interior, I complained about the very cold day.

"We can't do anything about the weather, Ardys. Too bad its so cold, but it won't bother all those kids from the country. They're tough, and a little below zero weather isn't going to keep them away."

We drove downtown, and he dropped me off on Sixth Avenue on the east side of Silver Lake. "Good luck," he said. "I'll pick you up at three-thirty at the Railway Station."

"Hey," he called, as he honked and backed up the car, "you forgot your skates."

An icy wonder world had been fashioned on Silver Lake. A flag-topped, ice facade entrance, which was flanked on the north by a 10-foot snow and ice statue of an American eagle carved by Philip Carlson of Virginia, greeted the contestants. A bump slide and a large, round, swivel whip sled called a Vipu-Kelkka, had been erected in the snow. About one-eighth of the lake was cleared of snow and covered with skating children waiting for their races to begin. I sat on a snowbank and put on my new, beige skates. I was confident that I would win, and only wished Carol were here to see me.

"Boy, it's cold," I thought when I had finished. I pulled my lucky mittens back on, tried to warm my hands by rubbing them together, and skated toward a warming shack near the edge of the lake. Various groups of musicians stood in clumps in the snowbanks serenading the spectators. Their gloved hands tried to warm their cold instruments, but strange sounds were heard as frozen keys and fingers reluctantly moved. Remembering the time I tore a piece of skin off my lips after putting them against the post of a chain link fence on an icy day, I wondered at their dedication.

The pot bellied stove in the warming shack welcomed me. The crowded room smelled of steaming wool and wood fire. I put my shoes into my rubber boots with the metal fasteners, and placed them under one of the benches around the perimeter. I tightened my new, beige skates. "I bet everyone wishes they had fast skates like mine," I thought, stretching my legs out in front of me to make sure they were noticed.

I had weak ankles. I didn't want to skate around the rink too much because my ankles would get tired and slow me down. But when I did start my warm up, it felt as though I had wings on my skates. I saw a few of my friends from my sixth grade class at Washington School, but most of the kids were older. Buddy LaLonde was doing figure eights in the center of the rink. I tried a few, but blamed my lack of success on the fact that I was a racer, not a figure skater.

I discovered I would be skating against girls in the 14 years and under classification. There were two races for girls. A 100-yard dash, and a 100 -yard dash, backwards. Not to worry; my skates were faster than Hans Brinker's. I had fogotten to practice skating backwards on my beige skates, but it couldn't be much different from skating backwards in my clamp-on roller skates in the basement of the Olcott Park house.

Bruno Cuppoletti, the Virginia Recreation Department director, blew a whistle, and boys eleven and under lined up at the starting line for the 100-yard dash. Recognizing Harold Allen, who was in my class, I yelled at the top of my lungs. "Come on, Harold. Faster. Faster." Donald Tekautz beat him by a hair, but Harold beamed when he was given his red ribbon.

"Girls fourteen and under for the 100-yard dash," the loudspeaker announced. Nervously, I skated to the start line. With heart pounding, and breath spewing clouds of fog before me, I dug

# The Winter Frolic

the point of my beige skates into the black ice. The blades sparkled in their newness, and my lucky mittens were toasty warm. I visualized them holding a blue ribbon.

The whistle blew. I took off. Body bent, I strained toward the finish, concentrating on watching my beige skates as they sped across the ice. Oh, I was fast. One hundred yards wasn't far. I was flying like a bird. Oh, no. The lace of my left skate came loose. My ankle began to wobble. My skate began to slip, and then I fell, ignominiously sliding on my prat toward the skaters who had already arrived at the finish. This couldn't be. I was too fast.

Ruth Rosemeier, Iris Michaels and Joyce Pladsen won that race and took home the blue, red and yellow ribbons, respectively. I pulled myself up, brushed off my snowpants, and watched as the boys twelve and over began their backwards race toward me. Bill Shimmin, Jack Finstad and Leonard Nelson were declared winners in a close race.

I felt like tripping Ruth Rosemeier, who skated backwards past me and toward the starting line. Instead, I followed her, watching how she did it. I turned around and tried it myself. It wasn't much different than roller skating backwards in the Olcott House basement. My beige skates could do anything. Maybe Ruth would fall. I wanted that blue ribbon, but I would settle for the red. Maybe, even the yellow.

"Girls 100-yard dash, backwards," blared the loudspeaker. The lineup was much shorter now; I would have a better chance of winning. No matter I had just learned how to ice skate backwards. I wanted that ribbon.

Ruth Rosemeier, Mary Ann Krebs and Iris Michaels took those ribbons home. I lagged far behind and couldn't believe it. They didn't even have beige racing skates.

Daddy met me later at the railway station. "Well, how did you do?" he asked. Throwing my not-so-fast, beige skates over my shoulders onto the floor of the backseat of the car, I said, "Don't ask. I didn't win. Carol will be disappointed in me."

"No one is disappointed in you, Ardys," Daddy replied. He squeezed my unlucky-mittened hands. "You tried. That's what's important. You had fun, didn't you?"

It had been fun, and I wasn't sorry I had raced. Next time, I would tie my skates tighter and practice skating backwards.

That night, we drove to the dedication ceremony for the Iron Bowl Winter Sports Center. Carol was layered with warm clothes and smelled of eucalyptus. Over 1,800 people crowded the bowl to watch the bonfires and fireworks of the Moonlight Frolic. Mayor Oscar Tamte and Judge Edward Freeman spoke, and members of the Junior Chamber of Commerce were hosts. Governor Harold E. Stassen sent his greeting to all the frolickers. Holding flares in their hands, a spectacular line of skiers dramatically flew over the ski jump in single file. It was seventeen below zero, but the excitement of the festivity warmed all who were there. The gallant Seabiscuit raced to win that day in 70 degree weather at Santa Anita Park in California in the $100,000 handicap, and on the same day, the hardy people of Northeastern Minnesota had a glorious, cold weather event that would also be long-remembered.

Waiting for Daddy, we stood by the warming shack and saw some commotion near the Vipu-Kelkka sled. Running over, we could see a young, curly-haired blonde boy lying on the snow, obviously in great pain. Doyne Anderson, thirteen, was the only casualty of the frolic. His leg was broken while pushing the whip sled with a number of companions after the tournament had ended. He was unable to get out of the way of the fast moving sled that traveled in a large circle around a center pole. He was brave and beautiful, and for the first time, I fell in love.

# The Winter Frolic

Mother and Daddy attended the Winter Sports Ball at the Memorial Recreation Building on First Street South later that evening. Mother, who loved to dance, looked so pretty and smelled so good when she kissed us goodbye. Aunt Aagie, our babysitter for the evening, made us popcorn. I was asleep before it was buttered.

It had been a very busy day. I dreamed of a girl with beige skates and dressed in blue ribbons who looked something like Ruth Rosemeier. The girl in my dream had curly, blonde hair and skated swiftly across Silver Lake with the laces of her beige skates trailing after her.

On Sunday, caravans of county school buses and autos arrived at City Hall, and the snow train shed its passengers in time for the rural men's bonspiel at the Curling Club. Tobaggan and slalom contests were held at the Iron Bowl. About 3500 people watched Virginia's graceful Martin Rukavina win the Class B ski jump tournament in the afternoon with two 126 foot jumps. Billy Anderson of Duluth had the longest jump of the tourney to win the Class A prize at 138 feet, an official hill record. Louis Colbasini of Virginia, and Clarence Hedloff of Ely, were also winners.

Drinking the cream of tomato soup Mother had put in my thermos, I gawked and oohed in awe as Kathleen Hughes, a Virginia Junior College student, stood on the top of the seventy-foot scaffold high above us. She twisted and turned her way over the ski jump for 80 feet to land on the 250 foot slope into the floor of the iron pit.

"Maybe I should trade my beige racing skates in for a pair of skis," I mused, as I watched her graceful jumps. A tiny, vivacious girl, she made it look so easy.

Meanwhile, at the Silver Lake Center, the rural kids were competing to determine their winter sport champions. In late afternoon, a J. Burt Pratt Post No. 239, American Legion- sponsored, fifty-unit parade marched down Chestnut Street. Tony Tranaas, its mounted parade marshal, led it from Railroad Avenue down Chestnut Street to the sports area on Silver Lake. A "Sundown" dance for snow train revelers at the warm "Rec" auditorium followed. Afterwards, Bertha Niskanen, queen of the Toivola Laskiainen Celebration, was crowned queen of the festival at the arena, followed by an Ice Follies presented by the Duluth Figure Skaters Club.

When the huge, black, steam locomotive returned to Duluth with its 900 tired, still-celebrating passengers at 10:00 o'clock Sunday evening, the platform was filled with Virginians waving them home. It had been some frolic. Even those of us who didn't sleep with ribbons under our pillows had fun. We had partnered with the frigid climate to revel in winter sports and appreciate the specialness of the northern ice land we called home. We were all winners.

### SKATING

When I try to skate, my feet are so wary
They grit and they grate.
And then I watch Mary, easily gliding,
Like an ice-fairy;
Skimming and curving, out and in,
With a turn of her head,
And a lift of her chin,
And a gleam of her eye,
And a twirl and a spin.

Herbert Asquith

# A PEEK INTO HISTORY

### Virginia Daily Enterprise

*February 23, 1940*
"Virginia will play host Saturday and Sunday to an estimated crowd of 10,000 winter sports enthusiasts during the sixth annual county winter frolic."
"It is being staged under the auspices of the Greater Rural St. Louis County Winter Frolic Association, the rural schools, civic and municipal organizations of Virginia and 100 rural community winter sports committees."

*February 27, 1940*
"Memories of Virginia's gala winter sports festivals of years ago were recalled Sunday as thousands of Duluth and rural frolickers crowded the city for the sixth annual county frolic."
"Winners in the Virginia junior events held Saturday afternoon included:
<u>Bump slide</u>: boys, 11 years and under—Billy Gilbertson, Jesse Gerulli, Dick Oakman; girls, 14 years and under—Ardelle Lofquist, Sharon Lenci, Clara Kilby; boys, 12 and over—Lee Wasson, George Biondich, Richard Lenci."

<u>Vipu-kelkka</u>: The team composed of Gloria Johnston, Joan Baland and Shirley Peterson tied for first place with the team composed of Kenneth Long, Willis Johnson, Bruce Barker; third place team—Ray Irish, Howard Olson, Richard Anderson."

## Superintendent's Reports to Park Commission

*March 31, 1939*
*"The Alpena Stock Pile, the Northside sports center, had a very popular snow slide. Later, with the help of the Gopher Club, a ski slide was constructed on the edge of Sliver Pit."*

*February, 1940*
*"The popularity of the Iron Bowl has been increasing by leaps and bounds. Every Saturday and Sunday we have had visitors from nearby towns including Tower, Ely, Cook, International Falls, Duluth and Cloquet. Almost every night you can find a group from Eveleth using the facilities.*

*"Two of the events held at the Iron Bowl were the highlight of the County Frolic. On Saturday night, February 24th, the Junior Chamber conducted the dedication ceremony. This was a colorful affair that has been the talk of the town for the past two weeks. The Park Department hauled in three large piles of old ties for bonfires and ordered a display of fireworks. The ceremony opened with a salute of serial bombs and rockets. Red, yellow and green fuses were placed around the Bowl, all along the ski landing and up the ski scaffold. Riders came over the jump with a flare in each hand. The actual cash outlay by the Park Department was $35.88. The crowd, estimated at 1800, was a good attendance, in view of the fact that the State Swimming Meet, a hockey game, and a dance and curling tournament were held on the same night. At least a dozen people called the park office to find out if this display would be put on again before the winter was over."*

*"The Winter Sports Club has laid out ski trails east of the Bowl. Last Sunday, two of the riders passed the word around that a*

*conducted tour of the trails would be held. Forty people turned out and were guided over the trails. These tours will start each Sunday at 1:30 from the Shadow Valley Club as long as there is enough snow for skiing."*

*"The facililties were maintained in good shape at the Iron Bowl during the month of February and there was no interruption in sliding during the month. Two outside toilets were constructed."*

*November, 1940*
*"Completed repairing the stairways at the Sports Project. The stairway railings had been stolen and rocks had been rolled down the steps."*

*"All loose boulders were removed from the walls of the pit near the sports site. One that was removed from above the bump slide must have weighed two tons and had to be moved off the runway with jacks."*

*"The International pumping unit was used to good advantage in icing the bump slides."*

*"A new, 8-year unconditional lease was procured from the Yawkey Estate. The government would not permit us to start the NYA Project until that was done. Some 200 yards of dirt were washed out of the ski landing during the summer. This will have to be removed."*

*December, 1940*
"As soon as the Christmas trees began to appear in the alleys, we began hauling them up to the Bowl. These are being frozen in along the tobaggan runways and bump slides."

*January, 1941*
"The long bump slide next to the tobaggan runway was completed. This gives us three good bump slides. Four downhill ski trails were constructed. The ski trail next to the Junior ski hill is used as much for tobaggan sliding as for ski sliding. We are going to build another bump slide along the South bank, which will be well protected from the sun. There was very little interruption in sliding during the month of January. We are trying to put the slides in such shape that they can be used as long as possible during the late winter."

"A new, straight tobaggan runway was constructed, which proved to be very popular during the winter."

"Total Winter Sports Project Equipment. $2,649.40 value includes tobaggan slides, 428' bump slide and Junior ski hill, ski slide, warming shack, two outside toilets, seventeen 7' tobaggans with pads."

*March 1941*
"Took down and cleaned up all refuse at Iron Bowl."

*January, 1942*
"Eleven loads of snow were hauled to the ski slide by the Park Department, the balance of snow required was hauled by the city."

*February, 1942*

"Several tobaggan parties were held in February and the attendance has been large, due to the warm weather. Our own men supervise the slide from 8:00 A.M. to 11:00 P.M."

*August, 1942*

"Large warming shack, which was partly under water, was dismantled and hauled into the park. All timber and lumber that was floating in the pit was picked up and hauled to the park storage area."

*August, 1942*

"If the water level continues to rise, we will have to abandon the Sliver Pit as a sports center."

*September, 1942*

"All material was removed from the sports center."

*Sons of Norway Floral Display*

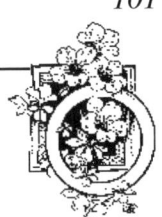

# CHANGES

On Sunday morning, December 7, 1941, Mother drove Carol and me home from the First Presbyterian Church where we attended Sunday School. Our chatter concerning the parts we were given for the Christmas program was in direct contrast to the cold, gloomy day. As soon as the maroon Lincoln Zephyr was parked in the garage, we ran into the house, through the kitchen and up the stairs to change our clothes and make our beds.

The Olcott House had been remodeled the previous summer and fall when, for a three month period, we lived in the "summer chalet," as Mother jokingly called it. The 25' by 40', one-room "refrectory building" adjoining the playground had a cement floor and high windows around its perimeter. There was a door on each end of the room. Its kitchen area contained a huge, gas stove with greasy, black handles that controlled the burner jets. A large, cut rock fireplace with Heatolater dominated the room and kept the center of it warm. Before we lived there, the wide counter was used for serving at lodge parties and wedding receptions, and the stains on the cold, grey cement floor testified to the building's popularity. On rainy days in previous summers, the playground director, Ida Canossa, used it for crafts. There was a toilet, but no bath. For that, we visited Silver Lake swim beach, and later, Mrs. Hakala, the feared inspector in the girls' showers at the Technical

Junior High School Swim Pool, spotted smudges of dirt on backs of necks and heels from three yards away. Mother supplemented with mandatory spit and basin baths.

To establish some kind of privacy, Carol and I created bedroom nooks, differentiated by our high, sleigh headboards and chests of drawers. Mother and Daddy had their own corner. Invariably, someone would get the giggles in the night causing all four of us to laugh in the dark over our temporary, homeless situation.

An evening ritual included saying goodnight to the several spiders who created and lived in intricate webs on the high ceiling. Wondering about the strange goings-on below them, they literally hung around to make sense of it. Mother spent long hours reading "Grapes of Wrath," and kept reminding us that "it could be worse."

Other uninvited visitors mistook the chalet for the public bathroom. One very young, lovestruck boy sat on his bicycle outside the door almost every day, waiting for Carol and me to appear. Sitting on the seat of his bike with his feet on the handlebars, he leaned against one of the posts on the cement porch that surrounded the building and peered into the chalet through an open, screened door. When one of us finally came out, he'd never say a word, but instead, would ride off and return the next day. We called him our guardian angel.

The remodeling was a definite improvement to the comfort and appearance of the Olcott House, and it was a happy day when we moved back. The stone pillars on each side of the front steps and its matching facing were removed and white siding was applied to the exterior of the house. The living room and upstairs front bedrooms were enlarged by raising the second floor and extending the house into the front porch area, and the narrow windows throughout the house were replaced. The kitchen was updated, but it was in the large, bright dining room where we played cards, talked with our friends on the telephone, and did our homework around the table. Monopoly was a popular new board game, and often on weekends, our cousins, Kitsy and Nancy, and Carol's friend, Lila Helland, would join us for a day-long game.

"Hurry, Ardys. It's almost time for the funny paper man," called Carol from across the hall. Even though I was almost a teenager and Carol was eleven, we always listened to the Katzenjammer Kids and Alley Oop comic strips read on Sunday afternoons on the radio.

Not having had a very large breakfast in our hurry to get to Sunday School, we went into the kitchen to make peanut butter sandwiches and get a glass of milk to tide us over until mid-afternoon when Mother served the proverbial Sunday chicken-in-every-pot with dumplings. Daddy was enjoying his second cup of coffee and reading the paper at the kitchen table.

"Well, my blondies, what are you planning to do for the rest of the afternoon?" he asked, as he pushed his chair away from the table and reached toward us for a hug. Carol scrambled onto one knee of his ample lap, and I rubbed the back of his neck with my sticky fingers.

Daddy was special. In the summer we spent many weekends at our cabin at Lake Vermilion where he taught us to run the motorboat, bait fishing hooks, swim, and shoot his twenty-two pistol at cans in the dump in the woods behind the cabin. The cabin was three miles by water from Moccasin Point where we left our car. If it was dark when we were on the water, we swatted at bats that swooped at our blonde hair.

One morning, just before dawn, Daddy woke us up to go down to the dock where we looked across the bay to where a moose with huge antlers was bathing in the water. The majesty of the animal and the peace of the morning, reflected in the calm waters of the large lake, made it an unforgettable moment for all of us.

Riding in the boat with him to a nearby island to get jugs of fresh spring water was a favorite excursion. We pretended we were landing on Plymouth Rock or did the "Dr. Livingston, I presume" bit. The cabin got its name, "Duck Shit Inn" because, upon reopening the cabin one spring, we found a dead duck in the living room. It had come in through the chimney of the pot belly stove and, very obviously, had been frightened out of its wits, and more.

I was now in junior high school, and Daddy encouraged me to take cello and declamation lessons and approvingly listened to my practices. He was civic-minded, gregarious and fun-loving and seemed to know everyone in town. Carol and I adored him.

"Well, it's about time for the funny paper man," Carol said in answer to Daddy's question, as she glanced at the clock on the wall. She moved from his lap and turned on the small radio that sat on the counter.

"*Gone With the Wind* is playing at the Maco Theater, Daddy. Would you give us a ride downtown this afternoon? We have to be there soon," I asked, while taking another bite of my sandwich. "Mother said we could go." Although released two years earlier, we had not yet seen the movie with Vivien Leigh, the English actress who played Scarlett O'Hara, and Clark Gable as Rhett Butler.

"Carol, turn up the radio," interrupted Daddy, suddenly getting up from his chair.

We listened as an excited announcer told of the surprise attack by the Japanese on Pearl Harbor at 7:50 A.M., Hawaii time. A large portion of the U.S. fleet, excluding aircraft carriers of which none were in the harbor at the time, was apparently destroyed or made inoperable. We were at war with Japan.

"Ink, come down here," Daddy called to Mother who had gone upstairs. "The Japanese have bombed Pearl Harbor. It's World War II."

Mother came running down the stairs and turned on the console radio in the living room. We hurried to listen to the announcer tell of the three attack waves of 360 Japanese planes that surprised the Hawaian naval base. There had been no declaration of war. They had bombed without warning.

Looking at Dante Tini's high school graduation picture, which sat on the mantle next to that of Grandma and Grandpa Hawkinson, with a catch in her voice Mother said, "Oh Carl, Dante is stationed on a ship in Hawaii."

Dante was the son of Daniel Tini, a long-time park employee. He had enlisted in the Navy after graduation from high school. We often had dinner in the happy Tini family home. My favorite was polenta, which we ate family-style on a platter placed in the middle of the dining room table. A little of Mr. Tini's home-made "dago red" was poured into small jelly glasses, half-filled with water for Carol and me. Afterwards, we enjoyed listening to the good looking Dante play his sparkling, silver accordian. Carol and I had secret crushes on Dante and agreed when he was home on leave after boot camp that he was about the best looking thing in uniform this side of Gary Cooper in Hollywood's *Sergeant York*.

Taking Mother's hand in his Daddy said, "Yes, you're right. Dante is in Hawaii. Well, let's hope he's all right."

Dante wasn't all right. He was killed that morning when a bomb hit his ship anchored in Pearl Harbor, Virginia's first World War II casualty. A gold star flag was hung in Mrs. Tini's window, and the beautiful accordian sparkled lonesomely in a corner of their living room. Mr. Tini, gentle and soft-spoken, continued to work faithfully at the park, but now, his ready smile was gone.

Most of the young men who worked on the park crews soon exchanged their shovels and hoes for guns and battleships. Daddy and Mother listened to H. V. Kaltenborn on the radio and worried about the progress of the war and their friends in the service.

Both Olcott and Southside parks had been enjoying a heydey of improvement and activity. In addition to the parks, the Iron Bowl, Municipal Golf Course, and all the city-owned outdoor properties and boulevards were under supervision of the Park Superintendent. More people used the facilities than ever before. The electric fountain in the rock garden, the annual begonia and chrysanthemum displays in the greenhouse, and the monkeys and other animals were viewed and appreciated by visitors from all over Minneosta..

One Sunday afternoon in the summer of 1942, the annual Hawkinson family reunion was held in the picnic area of the park to honor our cousin Buck, who was leaving for the Army. After eating Swedish beans, hot dogs, potato salad, jello, and lots of desserts to satisfy the family sweet teeth, we younger cousins ran off to see the monkeys. Mother and the aunts walked over toward the rock garden to see the floral display honoring the 50th Anniversary of the Sons of Norway that Gunnar Peterson had designed. Each of the five Hawkinson brothers had married girls of one hundred percent Norwegian descent, as their Swedish father had.

My father and his brothers sat on the benches and talked politics. They were all Republicans and didn't approve of many of F.D.R's. progressive policies in his New Deal. They were angry with him for the country's lack of vigilance at Pearl Harbor. They were fond of each other and seemed to enjoy the brotherly teasing and name-calling that went back to their younger days.

Cousin Buck was lots of fun, too, and teasing him was great sport for the younger cousins. Stalking him and his girlfriend wherever they walked that afternoon in the park, we were finally rewarded by catching them kissing behind the bushes. Comparing notes later, we giggled and speculated on kissing and love-making in general. It was several years before any of us would have any personal experience.

Many family picnics took place in Olcott Park that summer when goodbyes were said to loved ones; for some, these were last goodbyes. We started a victory garden near the compost piles across the road from the greenhouse where we grew lettuce, corn, cabbage, onions, carrots, beans and radishes, both red and white. Almost every yard in town had a similar garden. And sadly, because there was neither feed, nor manpower to care for them, one by one, the animals in the park were killed. Mother was soon preparing venison, rabbit, elk, buffalo, and even bear meat for dinner. Although meat rationing wasn't to begin until early the next year, in the summer of 1942 meat was already scarce.

The federally-assisted funding programs such as WPA and NYA, which were designed to give people jobs during the Great Depression, were discontinued. Daddy worried about the park's future. Most of the young workers had enlisted or been drafted, and the maintenance of parks, boulevards and a golf course was done with smaller crews. However, because of gas rationing, more and more visitors from all over the Range were spending their leisure time in near-by Olcott Park, which was crowded with people who came to watch the newly-built electric fountain.

Singapore, considered the strongest naval fortress in the world fell to the Japanese, and in Guadalcanal, a series of land and naval battles of unprecedented violence began. Daddy read the *Virginia Daily Enterprise* and his eyes held a worried look most of the time, even though his smile was as cheery as ever. He loved his job and the people who worked with him.

I came home from school one day to discover he had suffered another heart attack and was in the hospital. He was released after two weeks and warned to take it easy, eat no salt, and quit smoking the cigars he enjoyed.

Mother baked salt-free bread upon which he slathered sweet, fresh butter churned on the farm by my Grandmother. It wasn't long before he was hunting ducks and pheasants and seemingly, as strong as ever.

More troubling to him than his health was his concern over the war. He had served in France during World War I and had experienced war's horrors first-hand. His temper grew short, and his lectures to Carol and me about being "good" girls grew lengthier. Carol was twelve; I was almost fourteen. "Never go out with a boy who is older than you," he said to me one day. I thought it strange, for at the time, I didn't even know any older boys.

He had another heart attack and spent a longer time in the hospital where there was now a shortage of trained nurses and doctors. Mother had been volunteering as a Red Cross Nurses' Aide at the hospital and gave him personal attention during his stay there. She bought a hospital bed and put it in the master bedroom for when he came home to recuperate. I hauled my cello up the stairs to practice in his bedroom, where we also did our homework and read to him.

Mother's apparent concern about his health spilled onto Carol and me, but none of us talked about it. Instead, I carried a scary feeling in the pit of my stomach most of the time. Unlike my latest heroine, Ingrid Bergman in *Casablanca*, I became a worry wart. So much had changed.

Carol and I joined Girl Scouts and met in the Scout Room in City Hall for weekly meetings where we knit afghan squares, which somehow were sewn together and sent off to refugees. We bought 25-cent war stamps each week at school, and learned it took a long time to save enough for the $18.75 required for a maturing $25 EE Savings Bond. We peeled tinfoil from gum wrappers and rolled it into balls. We saved all of our cooking grease in coffee cans and brought it to Person's Grocery for recycling for the "war effort." In 1942, everybody had a ration book, and everyone "spent" ration stamps for sugar and gas.

One night I secretly "borrowed" a pair of Mother's precious silk stockings to wear to a party. I was grounded for a week. Nylons hadn't been manufactured yet, and the short supply of silk was mainly being used for parachutes for our fliers. After that, even on bitter cold nights, I vainly painted my legs with brown foundation and tried to draw straight seams down the backs. Mother bought a cigarette rolling machine and Carol and I cranked them out faster than she could smoke them. Real cigarettes were sent to the men and women in the service.

We learned to jitterbug and practiced in the basement. Our old, clamp-on roller skates now hung dusty on the wall. On consecutive weeks we stuffed our blouses with tissue and became Ingrid Bergman, Rita Hayworth, Lana Turner and Betty Grable, depending on the latest movie at the Maco or Granada theaters where they had upped their prices to fifteen cents for admission. Mrs. Miniver, with Greer Garson, won the 1942 Academy Award, and Abbott and Costello kept us laughing, even though the newsreels brought the reality of war closer than ever. Saturday night's "Your Hit Parade" on the radio was almost required listening for teenagers, and we swooned over Frank Sinatra with the rest of the nation's young women.

"Now, don't forget to pick up your new glasses after school, Ardys," reminded Mother as we hurried out the back door to catch the bus for Junior High School. It was March of 1943. I was now in ninth grade, and Carol was in seventh.

"I won't, Mother," I replied, throwing her a kiss. I had given Daddy, who was still bedridden, a kiss and a hug before coming downstairs.

I was excited. Our Virginia High School Blue Devils were playing that night in the final game of the District Basketball Tournament at the Rec Building. Almost everyone in town would be there, and we had a good chance of winning. Aunt Alice had stood in line for a long time to get us tickets. And, with glasses to correct my myopic vision, I would even know who had the ball. Now that I was in ninth grade, I was old enough to go to the high school Kit Kat Dance at the Rec after the game.

Our team won that night, and after the Kit Kat Dance, I went home with Nancy Sarff to stay overnight. When I got there, Dr. Sarff said that he would have to take me home as my Daddy was in the hospital again and was very sick. Mother was at the hospital, but Aunt Aagie and Uncle Tige, my mother's brother, were at the house with Mary, their new baby.

Carol crawled into my bed in the middle of the night. "I'm scared, Ardys," she said as she snuggled close to me. Her hair was damp with tears, and her feet were very cold. I scratched her back until she fell asleep and then worried to myself for a long time. I listened for the sound of Mother's car but finally gave in to a deep weariness that called me to sleep.

In the morning, Mother came into my room. Her eyes were swollen, and she looked tired and sad. It was snowing outside, and the house was cold. I began to shiver. She sat on the bed, gathered both of us into her arms and told us that our Daddy had died and was now in heaven. We huddled together and wept.

More changes, for soon it was moving day again.

## Virginia Daily Enterprise Editorial

*March 14, 1943*
*Carl M. Hawkinson*

"In a community which from its genesis has learned to hold the Hawkinson name in high respect, it comes as a shock to realize that death has taken Carl M. Hawkinson, superintendent of the city's park system. Though he had been seriously ill for some little time, occasional rallies gave cheer and hope that recovery was imminent—but it was not to be, and demise occurred last Saturday morning.

"Mr. Hawkinson has left the mundane scene at a time when his abilities were at their fullest flower, yet the impress of a busy and useful life is left for continuing good. In this legacy to a bereft family and kin, and to the city, he has followed in the footsteps of an eminent sire. He was the son of the late Mr. and Mrs. Andrew Hawkinson, sturdy pioneers here and on the Vermilion Range.

"The late Carl M. Hawkinson came to Virginia from Tower with his parents in 1894. Except for time away while attending the University of Minnesota, and employment with the government as a forester and surveyor on graduation, followed by participation in World War No.1, Virginia has been his home since his people established abode here. Park board membership, service as a school director and many other worthwhile contributions to the general welfare marked chapters in the life of the deceased.

Mr. Hawkinson was a sterling citizen, a good husband and father, and was well disposed toward all with whom he came in contact. He will be sorely missed."

## A FAREWELL

My fairest child, I have no song to give you;
No lark could pipe to skies so dull and gray;
Yet, ere we part, one lesson I can leave you
    For every day.

Be good, sweet maid, and let who will be clever;
Do noble things, not dream them, all day long:
And so make life, death, and vast forever
    One grand, sweet song.

Charles Kingsley

*Carl M. Hawkinson*
*"Daddy"*

# A PEEK INTO HISTORY

### Superintendent's Reports to Park Commission

*July 31, 1940*
"The second floor of the residence was raised five feet and new studs put in. The plaster and hardwood flooring was removed from the second floor and the partitions put in. The fireplace chimney was taken down to a point below the roof and the kitchen chimney removed entirely. All refuse and old lumber was hauled out as soon as it was removed."

*March 31, 1941*
"Park residence was completely remodeled and a new garage constructed, adjoining the residence. NYA help was used where possible."

*March 1942*
"We are very fortunate that our building program was completed, late in 1941. All new construction is out of the question for the duration of the war. We will have enough new equipment and repair parts to tide us over."

*July 31, 1942*
"Have arranged for three loads of wood for picnic grounds. More people have used the facilities in the parks this year than ever before. The playgrounds have had a very large attendance."

*Olcott Park House and Greenhouse
1942*

# WHAT'S HAPPENED SINCE?

World War II continued for two more years, until the summer of 1945. The house in Olcott Park, since 1994 has been the home of the Virginia Area Historical Society and Heritage Museum. It has been remodelled to accommodate the museum's many changing displays, pictures and artifacts. It is well worth a visit. Membership in the Society is reasonable and its newsletter is interesting and informative.

The animals of Olcott Park are gone; there is no zoo. Little Leaguers play in the field where elk and buffalo roamed. Flower beds fill Monkey Island. A new elementary school overlooks it now, but children still fashion armies of snow fairies in the snow. The electric fountain sends showers of color into the skies on balmy summer evenings during the semi-weekly band concerts in the pavilion. The greenhouse has added one more wing and still presents outstanding chrysanthemum and begonia shows for the public. A poinsettia show has been added. Throngs of people continue to visit the park and use it for their picnics and festivals.

The wooden train trestle spanning the northeast end of the lake has been torn down, with only vestiges of its beginning and end left as monuments to the "ten ten." The D.W.& P. station is now a bank.

The veins of high-grade iron ore that once gloriously fed the Mesabi Iron Range and mining company coffers are depleted. The earliest standard in the early days of mining was from 60 to 65 per cent magnetic iron, a standard later lowered to 51.50 per cent. The taconite now being mined is a rock bearing from 15 to 30 percent magnetic iron particles and is processed, formed into pellets, and shipped by freighter on Lake Superior to the steel mills of the East. In Virginia, two of the giant, open pits that can be viewed by tourists from observation platforms are the Oldtown Finntown Mine View at Second Street North near the eastern edge of the city, and the Rouchleau Mine View on Highway 53, just south of Virginia. Minntac, a division of USX Corporation, has mined taconite since 1967 at a 37,000 acre complex that stretches ten miles across the Mesabi Range northeast of Virginia.

Tourism remains a major economic influence, and both Minntac and the Soudan Underground Mine State Park offer interesting tours. Soudan's underground, one and one half hour mine tour will take you one-half mile down into the earth. Ironworld USA, located in near-by Chisholm, offers extensive information about the Mesabi's history. It includes a 2.5 mile excursion aboard an early 1900 trolley along the edge of the scenic Glen Mine to Mesabi Junction, an unique, outdoor exhibit with vintage mining equipment, a restored miner's home, and a 1930's railroad depot. Giants Ridge Ski Area near Biwabik has replaced the Iron Bowl as Northeastern Minnesota's premier winter sport destination.

After we both graduated from the University of Minnesota, my husband, an "older" Virginia boy who served in the Navy in the Pacific in World War II, and I married and moved to California. Not Hollywood. Five children and seven grandchildren later, we have enjoyed many adventures together in much of the world. We've sailed fjords in Norway, ridden elephants in Thai jungles, soared in a balloon over the African Serengeti, battled high winds on an icy Great Wall of China, portaged swollen Canadian lakes, driven roundabouts in England, and fed sharks while snorkeling off Moorea in French Polynesia.

But, for me, nothing—absolutely nothing—surpasses the exciting, beautiful, summer-green and winter-white memories of those love-filled, childhood years when I lived in the big, old house in Olcott Park.

ADDENDUM
# Virginia Tourist Camp

*Gunnar Peterson, Long-time Master Gardener
and Floral Designer
Olcott Park*

American Legion Floral Display
1937

At one time, tourists camped in Olcott Park. In 1925, Park Superintendent Alton Thayer wrote about the "Tin canner or automobile camper who had free wood, water, light and other accommodations. He's the fellow with the fliver, and that tent and all other necessities of life trapped on, who gets by for very little and leaves comparatively little in the towns in which he stops." He continued, "Free is passing and paid camping is in future."

In 1926, there were 4,770 out-of-state campers visiting Virginia. In Mr. Thayer's 1928 report, he wrote, "Still camping. Moved to abandoned deer park—still free." He also complained about the mess the campers left and how the park employees had to clean up after them.

Apparently, someone listened to him because, in 1930, eight one-room tourist cabins were built to welcome travelers to the city of Virginia. They were first located across Ninth Avenue from the park, near where the hospital is presently, and were later moved to the beach, on the northwest side of Silver Lake.

The cabins had hot and cold water, showers, indoor toilets, electric lights, shelves, one chair and "fancy cords on the curtains." In my research on Olcott Park at the Iron Range Research Center in Chisholm, I discovered some paper composition notebooks that had originally been placed in each cabin to invite comments from guests.

The Beckmans of Minneapolis wrote:
"We used the gas,
We used the showers,

We used the bed for restful hours.
We found this place both clean and neat,
Even the room with the hole in the seat."

Mr. and Mrs. Edwin Johnson journeyed from Boyd, Minnesota and wrote,"Your cabin was nice and clean. So is your park across the way."

An anonymous traveler said, "First cabin had NO spiders." On September 12, 1930, Mr. and Mrs. Pepper couldn't stay longer because "They don't like us Canadians as they wouldn't 'except' our money."

Several visitors commented that the shower was worth the price of the cabin. One suggested that there be two chairs, instead of one.

The H.W. Osgoods brought their three children from Kansas City, Missouri and poetically wrote:
"Lucky, Lucky, I will say,
To find a cabin like this upon our way.
We like to travel,
We like to roam,
But this is sure like Home Sweet Home."

Many honeymooners enjoyed their stay, including Mr. and Mrs. Henry Wayne who wrote, "Cabins are O.K. So was everything else." The G.C. Knolls of Minneapolis enjoyed their visit as it was "plenty cool outside, but hotsy-totsy inside."

All was not perfect, however. On September 26th and 27th, one lady suggested that the city provide a wood stove as "it is 39° today." Another suggested that all the cabins lacked was a radio.

The H.L. Bartelts of Minneapolis commented on the terrible beds and no dressers. The price was right, however, as they stayed two nights and wrote further saying, "Most cabins at $1.50 have only a bed, table and a few chairs. No bath or running water. Many have kerosene stoves."

Five days later, Mrs. D'Oconnor and son Jack from Bald Eagle, Minnesota found the beds to be "very comfortable." Several complained about the noisy trains in the night.

The practical Reverend and Mrs. G.K. Goodwin of Wanoka, Oklahoma suggested the city "place a shelf over the sink under the mirror and one over the hot plate." Looking for a bit of action, perhaps, one fellow wanted to bet "plenty of dough that Stanford beats Minnesota in the 4th."

Four additional cabins were built after that first summer, possibly in response to those several happy campers who commented on the "finest and best equipped Tourist Camp in the country." The B.B. Hesse family from Fort Madison, Iowa had "been from New York to Los Angeles, and from Portland, Oregon to Quebec, Canada, and we have found none better." When the new hospital was built, the tourist cabins were relocated near the beach at Silver Lake.

Sometime after World War II, the city of Virginia decided it no longer wanted to be in the tourist cabin business. The cabins were sold to private individuals, who moved them to other locations. One tourist cabin returned to the city in 1989, a joint project sponsored by the Virginia Soroptimists Club, the Virginia Rotary Club, and the Lee Anderson family. The tourist cabin is presently part of the museum complex at Olcott Park.

View of Olcott Park and Silver Lake, 1941

Roman Fountain
Donated by Katherine Roman in memory of her husband Joseph

# ACKNOWLEDGEMENTS

Felleman, Hazel, (Editor). *The Best Loved Poems of the American People.* Doubleday & Company, Inc. Garden City, New York. (1936).

Fesler, Hon. Bert, Judge of the District Court. *The Arrowhead Country Before it Became Famous.* Speech to the Minnesota Arrowhead Association, Duluth. (1938).

Fleming, J. H. *Odes of the Arrowhead.* W. A. Fisher Company, Virginia. (1929).

Richards, Carmen, (Editor). *Minnesota Skyline, Anthology of Poems.* The Lund Press. Minneapolis, Minnesota. (1953)

WPA Workers of the Writers' Program. *The Minnesota Arrowhead Country.* Albert Whitman & Co., Chicago. (1941).

The Virginia Daily Enterprise, Virgina, Minnesota.(1936-43).

Iron Range Research Center, Ironworld Discovery Center, division of the Iron Range Resources and Rehabilitation Board. (IRRRB).

LeRoy Guss, former park employee and Mayor of the City of Virginia.

Erik Peterson, former manager, Heritage Museum Olcott Park.

Harry Lamppa, Jan and Len Nelson,Virginia Area Historical Association volunteers.

Southside Park
1917

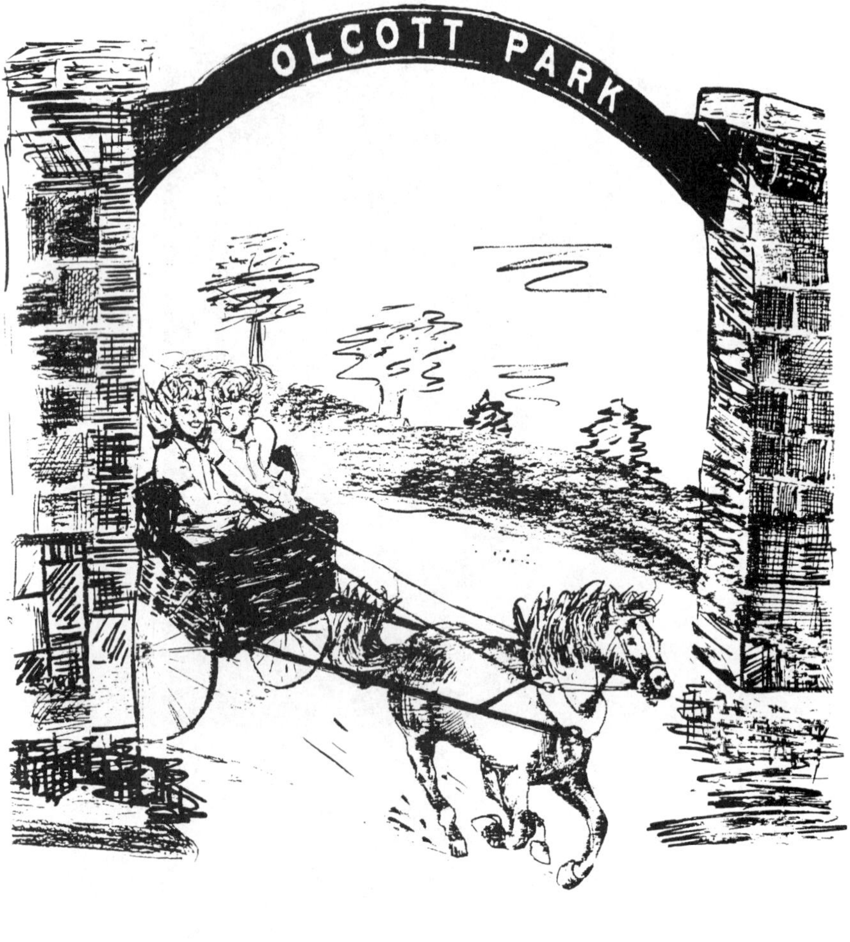
OLCOTT PARK

*Carol, Inky and Ardys Hawkinson, 1937*

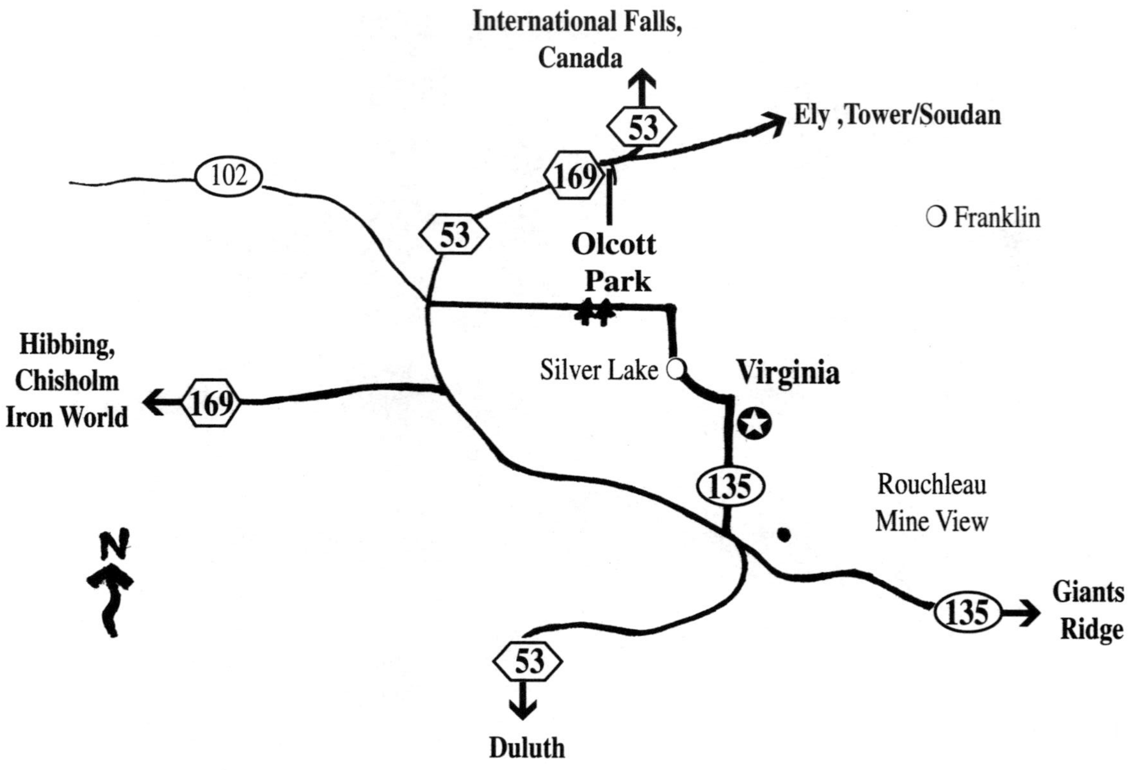

International Falls,
Canada
53
Ely ,Tower/Soudan
102
169
53
O Franklin
Olcott
Park
Hibbing,
Chisholm
Iron World
169
Silver Lake
Virginia
135
Rouchleau
Mine View
N
135
Giants
Ridge
53
Duluth